NO BETTER PLACE
TO DIE

Dropped behind enemy lines to protect Utah Beach on D-Day!

Robert M. Murphy

FOREWORD by Col. Mark Alexander

A

Combat!

Diary

CRITICAL HIT

First published in 1999 by Critical Hit, Inc.

A Combat! Diary is a trademark of Critical Hit, Inc.

Printed in the United States of America
International Standard Book Number 1-929307-00-4

Murphy, Robert M.
No Better Place to Die
1. World War II, 1939-1945—Unit Histories—France—Normandy

CONTENTS

{A photo section follows in the end of the book}

Psalm 23
The Shepherd's Psalm

The Lord *is* my shepherd; I shall not want.

He maketh me to lie down in green pastures; he leadeth me beside the still waters.

He restoreth my soul: he leadeth me in the paths of righteousness for his name's sake.

Yea, though I walk through the valley of the shadow of death, I will fear no evil: for thou *art* with me; thy rod and thy staff they comfort me.

Thou preparest a table before me in the presence of mine enemies: thou anointest my head with oil; my cup runneth over.

Surely goodness and mercy shall follow me all the days of my life: and I will dwell in the house of the LORD for ever.

INTRODUCTION

by Ian Daglish

We drive west out of a small French town. Passing under the new autoroute, we follow a minor road through quiet country-side. Two kilometers on, the hedgerows grow thicker and our road crosses a bridge over a deep cutting with a two-track rail-way. Suddenly we are in true bocage; the lane winds between high hedgerows. A final bend and the road straightens, sloping down past a large farm on our left. We stop opposite the farm buildings. Ahead, a river meanders slowly, flowing under the stone road bridge. Further ahead, beyond the bridge, our road turns slightly right to follow a raised road traversing 700 meters of open meadows. Through this tree-lined causeway and the hedgerows on the far side of the valley, we can make out the roofs of the houses and small church of the hamlet opposite.

All is peace and tranquillity. We have traveled hundreds of Kilometers to visit this site, yet there seems to be nothing re-markable here. The locals, most of them elderly farming folk, are unused to visitors, and stare open mouthed at the historian laden with cameras and camcorder, taken by surprise and curi-osity when he asks permission to film their homes and their farm-yards. Casual passers-by would see nothing here but tranquil, unremarkable French countryside. Unless they stopped where we have stopped, and read the small sign over a hole beside the road: 'Ici combattit le Gal. Gavin - 6 Juin 1944'. Unless they talked to the master of the Manoir, hearing his story and seeing his cache of antique weaponry. Or unless they have come upon the stunning memorial, the 'Iron Mike' statue at la Fiére. It stands as a sentinel of airborne troopers from bygone wars.

Monsieur Poisson ensures that no one is watching, then reaches his arm into the eaves of an old cattle shed. He pulls out an old mine, a grenade, the fossilized bag of a gammon grenade, its stockinette squares now stiff and its contact fuse rusted solid. It was one such grenade that the first American to approach the manoir on the morning of 6th June tossed in response to a German sentry's challenge. The German instinctively tried to catch the thrown object, and as the book puts it, "that ended for the moment the local resistance." Perhaps this was one of the grenades carried by men of the mis-dropped 507, who crossed the causeway after the battle for the *manoir* there, looking for friends and ran into German tanks. Or maybe this was just one of the many Gammon grenades whose owner gradually used up the "Composition C" plastic explosive charge, lighting tiny pieces to heat his coffee. In any case, the relic is a reminder of the days when this quiet valley was the scene of death and destruction, and a focus of the attention of the whole world.

For the distant town was Sainte Mere Eglise. The railway was an important rallying point for the mis-dropped regiments of the 82nd 'All American' Airborne Division on the night of 5/6 June. Where we stand stood Slim Jim Gavin, and General Matt Ridgway, and many more heroes of the 82nd. Opposite, the hamlet of Cauquigny was bitterly contested by the German 1057th Grenadier Regiment. And the causeway, then surrounded by deeply flooded marsh, was to change hands as both sides sought to win the strategic crossing. Captured by American soldiers at 1100 hours on 6 June, the la Fiére bridge was never again crossed by German troops.

Most of the tourists gathering in the summer sun in the busy little town of Sainte Mere Eglise have come to see a dummy parachutist suspended by his 'chute from the top of the church tower. They will visit the museum, buy some postcards, and leave for the Utah beaches, content that they have seen the key feature of the American paratroop landings. And they are right to think that Sainte Mere Eglise was the key to the Allies' right flank in the assault on Normandy. But in truth, the outcome at Sainte Mere Eglise was only briefly in question. By midnight on 6th

June, though Ridgway and his men did not fully realize it, the threat to their defense of the liberated town was over. It is at the bridgeheads, at Chef du Pont and especially the decisive battle at la Fiére, that the front line of the action was to be found, as the Merderet crossing became for four days and nights the focal point of both the German counter attack on the 82nd Airborne Division bridgehead and of VII Corps' westward advance across the Cotentin.

FOREWORD
by Mark J. Alexander, Col. USAR (Ret.)

Our country was at war. After years of warfare and planning, Allied forces were finally poised to mount the Normandy Invasion and free *Fortress Europa* from the Nazi yoke.

In the pre-dawn darkness of June 6, 1944 three Allied Airborne Divisions landed behind enemy lines, two in Normandy's Cotentin Peninsula. Their vital mission was to hold off the expected counter-attack by Rommel's panzer reserve against the Allied landing beaches. The 82nd Airborne Division was assigned the mission of protecting Utah Beach and ensure the exits from this American landing area would be free from enemy attack from the hinterland.

The specific mission of the 505th Parachute Infantry Regimental Combat Team was to seize the town of Ste. Mere Eglise, with its road and communications network. The unit had to prevent enemy forces from crossing the Merderet River and carrying out Rommel's plan to destroy the Allied landing on the beaches, where it was most vulnerable.

Low clouds led to the dispersion of the incoming C-47 troop carriers, scattering the parachute drops widely over the Norman landscape. Only the 505th RCT landed with any degree of accuracy, avoiding the movement of individuals and small groups seeking their parent units. This extra degree of cohesion was a good thing for the 505. The 1st Battalion, 505 RCT would soon be locked in a life-or-death struggle for control of the vital bridge at

1

la Fiére. German panzer and infantry forces struck hard at the defenders time and again. But at no time was the bridge to change hands until the "All American" soldiers handed it off to the American relief force, the men of the 357th Infantry Regiment, heading across the Merderet River from their landing-zone on Utah Beach.

Author and soldier Robert Murphy has done a commendable job in collecting numerous accounts from his fellow combat veterans, the paratroopers on the scene at la Fiére. This work provides a complete picture story of these events from the perspective of the combat soldier.

Chapter 1

SOLDIERS TELL THE TALE

I was among the fortunate paratroopers and glidermen of the World War II era 82nd Airborne Division that survived the war and returned home from Europe. 3,228 of my comrades were killed in action. Another 12,604 wounded in action. Most were killed in Normandy. Among the survivors, little was spoken or written by the average soldier regarding his personal combat experience. During the conflict his mail was censored by higher ranking officers. Few front line combat soldiers kept a diary memorializing their day to day combat experiences. The only written records were kept by the Division and Regimental headquarters staffs. These reports were prepared on a daily basis and are readily available at the U.S. National Archives in Washington D.C.

The U.S. Army Historical Division has a detailed and thorough summary of the Normandy battles by all Airborne and Utah Beach landing Divisions. These summaries named "Utah Beach to Cherbourg" were originally published in 1948 and provide detailed maps prepared by the Cartographic Division. These maps are phenomenal and priceless and selected ones are re-produced in this book. Many of the details on these maps come from officers that made personal notes and official entries in order to refresh their recollection years later when writing books or assisting military historians. These map records have great value in telling the story of the 82nd "All American" Division in Normandy.

3

But it was the low-ranking soldiers, the privates, sergeants and junior officers who fought the war in the front lines. These were the men who fired the rifles, bazookas and cannons and who were wounded and bled. They endured the cold or fever and lived from hour to hour, rather than day to day. These young combat soldiers were not taking notes or keeping diaries. They weren't writers or correspondents. Most were in their early twenties with no more than a high school diploma.

These men did not write about history, they made it[1].

A very detailed and, for the most part, accurate airborne history was completed immediately after the Normandy campaign. There are some errors which were made by the historians in that work that I shall correct herein. The U.S. Army History Officer, Colonel S.L.A. Marshall and his team interviewed the participants of the Normandy battles beginning with the 6 June Normandy jump and continuing through the 82nd's release from battle and return to England in May 1945. The Normandy combat narratives were recorded during late July and August of 1944—mostly taken from officers. These 'after action' reports were put into final written form by the Historical Section. These interviews, conducted within 60 days of the actual battle experience, are all part of the documented history and have been used as the basis for biographies and by authors who have written extensively about the Normandy battles.

Unfortunately, some authors who wrote about the battles in the area of *Manoir de la Fiére*, with its little bridge over the Merderet River, have made substantial errors. The material they researched was flawed or, most importantly, they never visited the scene of the battles or talked to actual participants. Some authors apparently do not know the difference between a bridge and a "bridgehead", as you will read below. The men in this documentary were deeply involved in the battle for the la Fiére bridge and the causeway running to the Cauquigny hamlet and its surrounding "bridgehead" area. It centers around men of the 505, 507, 508 and their courageous Regimental Combat Teams (RCTs) as well as the 325 Glider Infantry Regiment who came in by gliders on 7 June, D+1, between 0700 and 0910h (hours). In this work many eye-witness accounts are reported and corrections identified by Generals Ridgway and Gavin to the earlier recorded official history are also provided.

The readers of this historical documentary should clearly understand that it is not about the entire Normandy campaign. There have been scores of books written on World War II regarding all the Allied Forces in Europe as well as intimate details on the planning and execution of the armed forces assembled for D-Day. Two of the foremost airborne accounts are those authored by Lieutenant General James M. Gavin (*On To Berlin*) and General Matthew B. Ridgway (Ridgway's Memoirs: *Soldier*). My book specifically targets the mission of my Company "A", First Battalion, of the 505 (A/505) Parachute Infantry Regiment (PIR). The sole D-Day mission of Company "A" 505 was to seize and hold the la Fiére Bridge that spans the road west of Ste. Mere Eglise and runs over the Merderet River to Cauquigny and Amfreville. This account is about my comrades in arms and includes some stories of heroic members of the 507, 508 and 325 Regiments that fought with "A" Company in its assignment to take control of this particular little bridge against every weapon the German 91st Division and 100th *Ersatz Panzer Abteilung* could throw against them. Our time-frame spans June 6-9, 1944 but includes combat action by all 82nd units in the Ste.. Mere Eglise - Chef-du-Pont perimeter.

Because of my personal camaraderie and friendship with the men in my company, some may think their heroism tends to be overstated. Not so. The heroism of soldiers like PFC Lenold Peterson speaks volumes for itself. Peterson, a Minnesota immigrant Swede, was the bazooka gunner who stood up and knocked out two German tanks at a critical moment during the fighting at the causeway. His assistant, Marcus Heim, Jr, was by his side, along with their team-mates bazooka gunner PFC John D. Bolderson and his assistant Gordon Payne[2]. All these men should have received the Congressional Medal of Honor, but the army doesn't award that medal to four men at the same time. Peterson was nominated for the CMoH but another worthy hero that you will read of later in this work, Captain Dolan, never received a response to his July 1944 recommendation. In Gavin's book the author quotes a report by platoon sergeant William D. Owens in a footnote, describing the la Fiére battle and Owens' heroic part in saving the day there. In this work I provide more details on Sgt. Billy Owens, an older than average paratrooper who treated me like a young relative. I also have letters and tape cassettes

5

going back over thirty years, including correspondence with Owens, and others that were in the la Fiére battles. You will read of their noble achievements in the detailed eye-witness reports recorded by the Army History Section, along with signed letters from Captain John J. Dolan (A/505), Sergeant Owens and other battle participants that I have obtained personal reports and information from over the years. This is further supported by my own eyewitness recollection of these battles as a soldier in the first platoon of A/505.

The men of the 505 Parachute Infantry Regimental Combat Team (RCT)[3] were seasoned combat veterans with previous front line experience after parachuting into Sicily and Italy in July and September, 1943. None of the 507 Parachute Infantry Regiment (PIR) or 508 PIR (82nd) or the three 101st Airborne Division Parachute Regiments had seen any combat prior to the Normandy Invasion. The 101st Commander, Major General Maxwell Taylor, formerly with the 82nd, also made the combat jumps in Sicily and Italy in 1943.

Only the bare details of other Regimental assignments and D-Day missions are set forth herein. Each company in every regiment of both the 82nd and 101st Airborne Divisions had a specific target. I will only highlight and generalize those (other than 505 RCT) missions without providing lengthy details. Their missions have been well documented and recorded in other publications. In this historical work I will attempt to include what I think is important in one of the most vicious four day battles of the entire Normandy campaign. Certainly, the Chief Historian[4] who interviewed thousands of soldiers regarding many other European actions said that the battle at ".. la Fiére is probably the bloodiest small unit struggle in the experience of American arms." If you were not a participant in this historical battle you may choose to disagree with Army historian Marshall. If you took part in this battle I trust you will agree with him.

One must understand that there is a world of difference between the paratrooper and regular infantry soldier. The constant rigorous training of World War II paratroopers, their mind-set and fanatic attitude, as well as their boots, parachute wings and airborne shoulder patches set them apart from ordinary soldiers. There is a difference between men that jump out of airplanes into combat, miles behind enemy lines at night, compared to good

6

American or British soldiers who had the comparative *luxury* of landing on beaches as a cohesive unit with all their heavy artillery, tanks, supporting naval gunfire and communications. The D-Day paratrooper had only what he could carry in his musette bag and deep pockets. In Normandy he lost about sixty five percent of what was dropped with him from the C-47 aircraft in para-bundle containers. The best thing he had, besides his gun, was his attitude.

NOTES FROM CHAPTER 1:

1. I was 17 when I landed with the 82nd at Casablanca, Africa in May 1943 and just eighteen when we made the 505 Salerno, Italy combat jump in September 1943. By D-Day I was an 18 year "old timer". I did write home and still have every single letter I sent to my mother while in the Army, but very few detailed actual combat information.

2. Marcus Heim, Jr. from New York and Gordon C. Payne from California are both living. Peterson and Bolderson are deceased although they survived the war. All four received the Distinguished Service Cross, second only to the Congressional Medal of Honor.

3. The 505 Team consisted of the 505 Parachute Infantry Regiment, the 456 Parachute Field Artillery Battalion, Company B 307 Parachute Engineers, 80th Airborne Antiaircraft Battalion and 307 Airborne Medical Company.

Chapter 2

A CHANGE OF PLANS

Substantial changes to the entire mission and Drop Zones (DZ) of the 82nd regiments were made only ten days prior to D-Day. The original 82nd Airborne Division paratroopers of the 505, 507 and 508 had Drop Zones that were to the west of the Douve River near Ste. Sauveur Le Vicomte. The three regiments were assigned to occupy the town and the surrounding hills and clear the way for the glider landings at dawn and during the evening of D-Day.

They were also tasked with stopping German tanks and division-size troops from moving eastward, toward Utah Beach. For months, those missions were planned in every detail and set to go on 30 May, the original D-Day. The original airborne plan was suddenly canceled on Friday 26 May; for good reason. Air reconnaissance photos showed many tiny holes in the open fields and slices of earth dug out of hillside roadways. This was done to park and protect German army trucks and vehicles from the incessant Allied fighter and bomber attacks. The tiny holes in the ground were, in fact, utilized to place tall poles (called *Rommelspargel* or Rommel's asparagus) interconnected with grenade laden wire to defend against airborne and glider landings.

The Enemy

By June, 1944, the Wehrmacht had evolved sophisticated doctrine for opposing airborne assault. Said SS Captain Krafft, 'The only way to draw the tooth of an airborne landing, with an inferior force, is to drive right into it." The German 91st *Luftland* (air-landing) Division (for 'air landing', we should read 'anti-air' landing) with its 1057th and 1058th Infantry Regiments, artillery and tanks had just moved in, using Ste. Sauveur Le Vicomte as its division headquarters. The 91st was under the command of General Wilhelm Falley. Though only an ad hoc, improvised unit (formed in 1944 in *Wehrkreis* XII around Wiesbaden), and thus poorly equipped, the two infantry regiments of the 91st were nevertheless to have a major impact on the development of the American airborne bridgehead. Indeed, identification of this newly arrived division in May led to major revisions to the planned 82nd drop zones, mere days before Overlord.

As reports of the airborne landings came in to the German Seventh Army headquarters and the extent of the landings became apparent, General Dollmann ordered a series of moves designed to seal up and destroy the airhead. The units ordered to oppose the paratroopers consisted of the 1057th Regiment (91st Division) and the 100th Panzer Replacement Battalion. By means of concentric counterattacks Dollmann was sure at first that he could cope with the Cotentin landings without moving in any additional forces. It was only during the evening of June 6 that his optimism waned, as the 91st Division reported that its counterattacks were making slow progress because of the difficulties of maneuvering in the hedgerow country. In reality, the attack had scarcely materialized at all except in local actions along the Merderet.

The lack of success of the German D-Day reaction by the 91st Division can be partially explained by the loss of its divisional commander. *Generalleutnant* Wilhelm Falley was away from the battle-front, along with some of his subordinate commanders, attending a war game at Rennes. Upon his return, Falley was promptly killed by paratroopers.

Division and Regimental Missions

New orders came down to the division: cancel the original 82nd mission and formulate a totally new airborne plan for all its regiments. A new plan was formulated in less than ten days time. An entirely new target was picked for the three 82nd Airborne parachute regiments and their incoming glider landing force. The new plan called for both the 507 and 508 Parachute Infantry

Regiments to drop west of and astride the Merderet River and block the German 91st Division from attacking to the east. The 505 PIR was to jump east of the river and capture the town of Ste. Mere Eglise, a known German anti-aircraft headquarters area. The plan also called for the seizure of the two outlying bridges crossing the Merderet River at la Fiére and Chef-du-Pont.

The final 101st Airborne Division D-Day mission remained similar to its original plan. The 'Screaming Eagles' were to jump east of Ste. Mere Eglise in order to open and clear the four critical Utah Beach raised road exit causeways in an area of flooded marshland, below road level. The 4th Infantry Division, landing at Utah Beach, had the task of getting up, over and through the causeway exits leaving the beach. These exit roads were cleared by the 101st paratroopers after many sporadic and tenacious small group battles with enemy rear echelon and beach front defenders.

The 4th Division, led by the 8th Infantry Regiment, and followed by the 746th Tank Battalion, actually landed south of its intended landing area. The U.S. Navy ships and low-flying aircraft laid down such a terrific bombardment on the beach front before 0630h, that the pilots of the landing craft could barely make out the beach with the dust raised by bomb blasts. The tide also carried the 4th south of its intended landing zone. Nevertheless, the unit got ashore quickly and with a majority of its equipment intact. Just the opposite was true at the Omaha Beach killing ground. There, confusion, death and devastation reigned all day.

Merderet Marsh Tragedy

On the west side of the Merderet River running about 8000 yards north and southeasterly between the la Fiére Bridge area, the entire prairie was flooded and inundated by the Germans by closing the La Barquette Locks in 1943. The flood-water went undetected by American photo and map experts as reeds, tall grass and rushes grew up out of the immense new marshland. These treacherous waters claimed the lives of many 82nd paratroopers as well as tons of weapons and ammunition dropped in para-containers. The DZ selection for the 507 and 508 Regiments was one of the worst and tragic mistakes by Allied pre-invasion strategists who merely forecast this new wide open prairie drop zone as "..ground here probably soft". The Germans couldn't conceived a more deadly trap.

Almost all of the 82nd paratroopers, including Major General Matthew B. Ridgway and Brigadier General James M. Gavin were without any working radios on D-Day. There was little or no contact or "walkie-talkie" radio communication between regiments or down to the squad level. There was absolutely no contact by the 82nd commanders and the Utah Beach landing force until 2100h on the evening of D-Day. General Ridgway finally got a working radio and spoke in the clear to the 4th Division requesting immediate supplies of ammunition, medical aid and tank support and plainly stating, "Get your tanks through to Ste. Mere Eglise."

Most 507 and 508 troopers landed after 0214 hours on June 6th and were totally scattered, unable to attack or defend as functioning cohesive battalion and company-size units. The 507 and 508 landed, for the most part, all over the west side of the Merderet River (82nd) DZ areas. Some of the more fortunate 508 men were mis-dropped on the east side of the swamp and joined the 505.

The 101st paratroopers were also mis-dropped in small units near Ste. Marie Du Mont, also north of the La Barquette locks, and around the Ste.. Germain de Varreville district. The few 506 PIR (101st AB) men that landed in or near Ste. Mere Eglise immediately made their way to the east in the direction of the 101st Utah Beach causeway exit assignments. Most paratroopers of the 101st (except the 3rd Battalion of the 506 PIR) were gathered in small units consisting of 5 to 100 men in the area west of and behind Utah Beach and north of Carentan. No matter what regiment men were assigned to before the jump, they fought that night and day with whatever unit they ran into, whether in a force of 5, 10 or 100 men under the command of an officer or sergeant.

Except for the 505, these small knots of the 82nd and 101st troopers were dropped in the wrong place. The unfortunate C-47 aircraft pilots had minimal training for their task, leading to the mis-drop of most 507 and 508 pathfinder units. Matters were made worse by the cloud cover encountered along the flight path at 600 to 900 feet altitude as the pilots approached their assigned drop zones. Some of the pilots, after missing their assigned DZ, turned around and dropped their men on the way back, getting shot at both ways. Other pilots, shaken by anti-aircraft fire, failed to slow their C-47 aircraft. Jumping at 150 knots, a trooper had much of his equipment ripped off his body or was injured before he even hit the ground. Despite all the hardships, some craft were piloted by experienced pilots like Colonels Joel Crouch and Charles H. Young and succeeded in putting their men dead-on their drop zones.

The 505 Pathfinders[5] were made up of highly-trained combat veterans. Their experience was augmented by senior U. S. Air Corps pilots with whom these men trained since November 1943. The end result was the great majority of the 505 PIR landed on their drop zones. The unit had by far the best drop of all the regiments of the 82nd and 101st Airborne Divisions.

The 505 Parachute Infantry Regimental Combat Team mission was to take and hold Ste. Mere Eglise by the morning of D-Day and set up a road block on the main highway north of town, near Neuville au Plain. Additionally, their orders were to seize both of the small Merderet River bridges at la Fiére and Chef-du-Pont. The 507 and 508 troopers were assigned to jump on the west side of the Merderet River (northeast of Amfreville and Picauville) and block the enemy from advancing over these extremely important river crossings or into the town of Ste. Mere Eglise. In that mission, they failed that night. The 507 and 508 did not complete their missions, in the main due to mis-drops. They fought on as scattered units wherever they landed. Despite the darkness and the mis-drops, many of the men reached the la Fiére and Chef-du-Pont bridges.

General Confusion

The unfortunate D-Day pre-dawn disposition of eighty percent of both the 82nd and 101st Airborne Divisions' paratroopers curtailed their effectiveness. They could not fight as battalion or regimental-sized attack forces until the men could locate and return to their units. Regrouping to at least battalion-size took almost two days. Some platoon-size units were isolated even longer, some for four or five days. All of this unintended dispersion had one advantage. Before daylight the Germans reported to their respective superior headquarters, leading all the way up the chain of command to Berlin, that paratroopers had landed over a twenty-five square mile area on the east side of the Cotentin Peninsula. This supposedly widespread drop area confused the enemy. They had no idea the paratroopers were mis-dropped; or how many they faced. The magnitude of the airborne invasion force was a mystery. Thus, the German reaction was slow and uncertain.

Despite the confusion, the German war machine quickly responded in the pre-dawn darkness and after sunrise on D-Day. The first response was to engage the paratroopers and glidermen in each unit's immediate vicinity. Hundreds of small firefights broke out amidst the bocage, resulting in many deaths on both sides before the Allied beach landings at 0630 hours.

Before daylight the 82nd Airborne Division was reinforced at 0400h by 52 gliders transporting men of the 80th Airborne Anti-aircraft Battalion (Batteries A & B), some 82nd Division Artillery, 82nd Division Signal, and Headquarters staff with 57mm anti-tank cannons, antiaircraft weapons, radios, jeeps, trailers and extra ammunition. Many of these heavily-laden gliders crashed in the small hedgerow fields and sank in the swamps. Many a gliderman and paratrooper died this way and a loss of cargo trapped inside the wreckage of the gliders resulted. General Gavin himself, mis-dropped with the 508 PIR, spent considerable time attempting to recover a jeep and 57mm cannon out of a crashed Waco CG4A glider west of the Merderet River in the flooded grassy marshland. Intense enemy fire drove Gavin and his men from the effort with no success in extricating the valuable armaments. Gavin's little group quickly returned to shore with a wounded paratrooper they encountered in the marsh. Mission "Elmira" would later land 176 British Horsa and Waco gliders on D-Day during daylight hours at 2110h and later in the darkness at 2300h. The rest of the 80th AAA Battalion went to Normandy on Liberty ships and by 8 June Batteries "D", "E" and "F" had transferred to LCT's with the bulk of the jeeps, small 1/4 ton trucks, trailers all backup equipment and tons of cannon ammunition.

Ste. Mere Eglise was the first town in France to be liberated. It was captured by the third battalion of the 505 by 0430h on June 6th. The second battalion 505, and notably one heroic "D" Company platoon of 47 men led by Lt. Turner Turnbull (killed in action the next day) was moved into a perimeter protecting the north side of the town near Neuville au Plain on the Cherbourg-Carentan main highway at 1030h. The third battalion then defended against entry into the town from the south. The first battalion 505 fought along both sides of the roadway directly approaching the vicinity of the Manoir de la Fiére bridge area. By 1030h the bridge and adjoining rugged stone residence and barn buildings had been seized and all German defenders killed or captured.

Company "A" of the 505 PIR assembled almost ninety-eight percent of its men under the leadership of its tenacious, hardnosed first lieutenant John J. 'Red-Dog' Dolan (Dolan had red hair). Its sole D-Day mission was to seize the la Fiére bridge and hold it so that the armor of the 4th Division and the 8th Infantry Regiment plus heavy artillery, could cross it to head to the west. "A" Company 505 did just that. Once the unit and some supporting 507 and 508 men had command of this little bridge by 1030h on D-Day, no German crossed it again, except as a prisoner of war.

The west side of the so called "bridgehead" at the Merderet River was anchored at the small hamlet and old church of Cauquigny, approximately 750 yards (250 meters) from the la Fiére crossing. The "bridgehead" consisted of the area between Cauquigny, running east across the raised causeway, to the bridge and its adjacent Manoir. Some authors, unfamiliar with and ignorant of this battlefield, have confused the actual bridge and "bridgehead" locations. In military parlance, the bridgehead was the entire area around and east of Cauquigny. This area extended over the la Fiére bridge at the foot of the Louis Leroux family home (the Manoir, or manor house, a substantial Norman stone structure) and farm buildings, called the *Manoir de la Fiére*. The Manoir is not to be confused with the hamlet and chateau estate buildings, also named la Fiére, which are 1000 yards northeast near the Merderet river road and the railroad tracks. When soldiers and authors refer to "la Fiére" they mean the little bridge and the Leroux Manoir de la Fiére; not the little hamlet unless, specifically referring to this other area.

NOTES FOR CHAPTER 2:

4. S.L.A. Marshall, Brig. General (ret.) U.S. Army, author of the bok "Night Drop" (1962) and many other books on military history. The official U.S. Army (public record) history of Normandy about this battle is amply quoted.

5. Including author of this documentary Robert M. Murphy. The Pathfinders were hand picked, 3 men from each company who had double duty to train as infantrymen but also jump ahead as Pathfinders with lights and radar/radio beacons. Finishing that job they returned to fight with their regular unit.

Chapter 3

OPERATION OVERLORD

The 82nd Airborne Division paratroopers and glidermen had been moved from their camp training grounds in central England to the various major airfields at the end of May. They were sealed in without leave, telephone or outgoing mail. Massive hangers were emptied of aircraft and cots were set up for the men. The usual rumor mongers actively spread invasion fables, while poker and crap games flourished. Food was served with 75 yard chow lines and everybody wrote letters home or to new girlfriends from Leicester, Loughborough or Quorn where we had our 505 PIR 'tent city' camp.

At least 75 percent of the men of the 505 Parachute Infantry Regiment Combat Team were combat veterans. They knew exactly what to expect: incoming mortar rounds, the terrifying German 88's, machine pistols (burp guns) and one-on-one attacks against machine-gun nests. The problem now was the "waiting game". Troopers who knew the probability of getting killed or getting an arm or leg blown off experienced nervous anxiety and tension. They had seen 'it' happen to their comrades in Sicily within the previous year; so death and injury was not fiction to these men, but fact. The few days leading up to the expected take off night of June 4th were rather fitful and disquieting. We had all of our weapons, ammunition, grenades and K-rations as well as everything we could pack in our jump suit pockets and musette bag backpack. Only combat necessities were stuffed in the gas mask bag including gum and candy. Without the gas mask!

When the invasion was actually called off on 4 June and postponed one day the great majority of troopers breathed a sigh of relief. The fear of being killed or horribly wounded in action was washed out of their minds and a sense of relief pervaded our airborne invading force. The old banter, kidding and games were back in place as the order of the day during the morning and afternoon of June 5th. Although we knew we were going to Normandy within a matter of hours, there was a great mood change. The old 505 mind-set—'airborne'—was back. The men were now more than ready after the pressure was somehow turned off the day before June 6th.

Operation *Overlord* was postponed by General Eisenhower on June 4th due to high seas, making it impossible to land the 170,000 sea-borne invasion troops at all the separate American and British beaches. Part of the invasion force had already embarked when a full blown storm struck the English Channel and Normandy beaches. Eisenhower, while the weather was still miserable, made the final commitment to "Go" at 2145 hours on 4 June. The full force of the second front invasion was now in motion. The ships and landing craft of every type were pointed in the direction of Normandy.

The Germans were so sure that the famed warrior, Lieutenant General George S. Patton, and his make-believe imaginary Army was supposed to invade in the coastal Pas de Calais area they had it strongly defended by the German Fifteenth Army. They had top-notch panzer and infantry divisions waiting to strike back in Pas de Calais, the closest landing-beach between England and France. The Allied scheme that fooled the Germans was called operation "Fortitude" and included actual Air Force bombings, intense radio traffic, silver foil drops to choke off radar signals and other disruptive measures. "Fortitude" worked like a charm because at 0730h on D-Day, 6 June, Field Marshall Gerd von Rundstedt called Berlin and requested the immediate movement of two reserve Panzer Divisions (the 12th and the 21st Panzers) to counterattack in Normandy as rapidly as possible. He was denied the use of the panzer reserve. General Alfred Jodl, in Berlin, did not wish to wake Hitler to ask his permission to release the panzers. As has oft been recorded and discussed by historians since the event, this armor could have started out for Caen

17

and the Omaha Beach areas without getting attacked by Allied daylight fighter planes due to the cloud cover. Nothing was in their way to stop them until they hit the oncoming Allied invasion beach force. German blunders and failure to immediately commit this powerful force was the beginning of the end of the Third Reich. It was just a good break for the Allied combat soldiers on the ground. It was not until 1600 hours D-Day that permission was finally granted by Hitler to utilize the two panzer units sitting idly on stand-by.

Back at the 82nd and 101st Airborne Division paratrooper airfields, serious business was taking place just outside the jump aircraft. Each trooper was responsible for the equipment and weapons he carried into combat. When he jumped from the C-47 aircraft in the dark over Normandy he took only enough gear to raise havoc with the enemy. And his courage. Most men had to be helped up the steps into the C-47 because of the tremendous weight of the combat material compounded by the heavy rear parachute and the reserve parachute in the front along with his Garand M1 rifle carbine or .45 caliber Thompson sub-machine-gun. The pathfinders had all that gear plus the extra thirty pounds of radar and radio beacon equipment and batteries for the light team.

The 505 PIR had officers that had acted as jump-masters over combat targets in either Sicily or Italy. They were cautioned to use extreme care to look at the approach geography and look for the Drop Zone and Pathfinder lights. And be damn sure you know where you are before you yell, "Let's Go". They were aware of the frailties of the young and inexperienced C-47 pilots and separate navigators going through anti-aircraft fire and the probability of their flying an avoidance detour, off course. In fact, Lieutenant Colonel Ben Vandervoort, 2/505, looking out the door passed the word back to tell the pilot to shut off the green "Go" light because he was no where near the 505 DZ. Highly trained jump-master officers and sergeants, with their heads out the door studying the terrain below, were determined to get to their DZ. From their drop experience in Sicily they knew the consequences of a scattered regimental combat jump. Thanks to the Air Corps 315th Troop Carrier Group flying 600-700 feet, in 'ack-ack', they got the 505 PIR a near perfect drop with only a few scattered men who were able to join up with the regiment by mid-morning

The Battle at la Fiére - First Battalion 505 PIR Mission

About 800 yards east of the Merderet River and Manoir de la Fiére is a double tracked rail line running from Cherbourg to Paris. At this intersection there is a bridge above the tracks. It was usual for the Germans to post guards on such bridges and to have soldiers walking the tracks. This main roadway and rail track intersection became one of the famous landmarks and focal assembly points for the widely dispersed 507 and 508 paratroopers, including Brigadier General James M. Gavin, the 82nd assistant division commander who dropped a mile off course with the 508 PIR.

There were regular German guards posted on and near this railroad bridge intersection that June 5th night. What was more phenomenal and a stroke of bad luck for the 82nd paratroopers in general, and the 505 first battalion in particular, was the assignment of a platoon of Germans posted in and around the M. Louis Leroux Manoir farm building and bridge. Monsieur Leroux later told historians that twenty eight German infantrymen got him out of bed at 2300 hours on 5 June and told him they would be outposting his property. He said he was amazed as no soldiers had ever guarded the la Fiére bridge or Manoir before that night.

While the enemy was thus settling in around the Manoir and bridge, the 505 was airborne and well on its way heading for the English Channel. So it was, 878 years after William the Conqueror left Normandy sailing for England with 13,000 fighting men, we also had, on 5 June 1944 at 2300 hours, 13,000 paratroopers heading for Normandy, and 146 of them straight for Louis Leroux's farm house. They jumped at 0151h on June 6th.

Each battalion of the 505 PIR had its specific mission. The men immediately formed up in battalion strength. The only thing missing that night were some of the para-container bundles that may have overshot their landing area. The rule was to take any bundle you found, take everything inside and later on, after finding the rightful owner of the light machine-gun, 60mm or 81mm mortar, bazooka or ammunition and make the swap. A machine-gunner who found a bazookaman would later swap weapons and vice versa.

By dawn almost every 505 trooper had the right equipment plus the recoverable weapons and jeeps brought in at 0400 hours by the 80th AAA and 82nd Division Artillery gliders. Several by the 80th AAA and 82nd Division Artillery gliders. Several God-sent gifts like the small 57mm artillery cannon were hauled out and put to excellent use against the German tanks of the 1057th and 1058th Grenadier Infantry Regiments and tank battalions of the 91st Division. The 57mm cannon is like an oversized rifle. It is very accurate and can be fired from a short or medium distance. The trouble with firing a 57mm was that when you have the enemy in sight, so they to have a line-of-sight to you. The guns generally did not stay hidden behind the hedgerows long. It was situated out front where the crew (or any soldier) could get a direct shot at a tank or opposing cannon.

Corporal Francis C. Buck, Headquarters Company First Battalion 505 PIR was in the same plane with the Battalion commander, Major Frederick Caesar Augustus Kellam. After landing on the DZ, Major Kellam had Frank Buck set up the 1/505 assembly light. On leaving the DZ, they moved along the road and at the hamlet of la Fiére (not the bridge and Manoir area) they saw a light on in a house. Major Kellam had a French speaking trooper get specific directions from a rather frightened, but elated farmer who pointed to the la Fiére Bridge and Manoir. Some mention was made by the farmer that there may be Germans on the railroad and by the road crossing. Kellam had not located his Executive Officer, Major McGinity (who was with "A" Company) so his group moved out heading for the first battalion objective, the la Fiére bridge. They were right on time and only a few hedgerows away from Red Dog Dolan and "A" Company.

First lieutenant John J. Dolan, the "A" Company 505 PIR commander, code name Red Dog, was a veteran of the early 505 misdrop in Sicily and had ordered a training program on night time parachute assembly. Assembly was the key. He was law school trained[6] and an aggressive combat leader who didn't say too much. But when he did converse, it was worthwhile to pay attention and follow his orders. He was one of the best, a combat out-front leader, not a follower.

Dolan and his company had the best assembly of *Operation Neptune*. They landed about 0200h right on the edge of the 505 1st Battalion DZ and soon after, Dolan approached the pathfinder team. We (the author) talked about the terrain, where the railroad tracks were, the la Fiére bridge, and the east-west road, a probable location for enemy action. The officers gathered around

Dolan while the "A" Company men put their weapons together and secured the para-bundles containing our 60mm mortars, bazookas and ammunition boxes for the .30 caliber light machineguns. Everyone seemed exuberant, high spirited and ready for action. There is a peculiar elation, a feeling that paratroopers experience after combat jump. Their chute opened, they reached the ground, alive. That particular joy was manifested by my training-camp tent-mate, Corporal Darrell Franks. He came looking for me to ask if I saw our squad Sergeant Bill Owens, which I had. Darrell, a good-old-boy from Ashville, North Carolina, jokingly said "Hey, Moy-fee (Murphy) have you seen any of those Vou-lay Vous cooshares tonight?" I never forgot that question and I leave the reader to interpret the famous words most young paratroopers wanted to learn in French. At least this facetious remark by Franks was proof of a spirited and not a fearful mood.

Lieutenant Dolan requested that P.F.C. Charles Burghduff of "A" Company (who jumped as a pathfinder) go with the entire company, because he spoke German. Dolan knew exactly where he was within 20 minutes of landing. He ".. was able to identify a "T" intersection, dirt roads 8 to 10 feet wide, near our drop zone. The upper arm of the intersection ran generally east to west; the vertical arm ran north to south, to meet the road running from Ste. Mere Eglise to our objective—the bridge at the Merderet River."[7]

"A" Company moved out from the drop zone an hour before dawn along the north-south dirt road heading for the bridge. Dolan ran into Major James McGinity (the executive officer who was second in command of the 505 First Battalion) who joined the march with "A" Company. McGinity told Lieutenant Dolan that he had discussed the good jump assembly and map location with the 3rd Battalion Commander, Major Edward C. Krause, who was already formed up and heading east to immediately attack the German occupied town of Ste. Mere Eglise.

Here's Dolan's account of the events at this time: "The "A" Company.. first platoon order of March was Company Headquarters, third and second platoons. When we reached the road running east-west from Ste. Mere Eglise, a German motorcycle passed us going toward Ste. Mere Eglise. At this time it was still dark but daylight was starting to break. We crossed the road and started west toward the bridge, with a hedgerow to our right, between us and the road. Just about this time, contact was lost with the first platoon, so the third platoon took the lead."

"About seven to eight hundred yards from the bridge, we came upon a dirt road running southeasterly from the road to the bridge. Hedgerows were on either side of this road. Beyond the road in the direction of the bridge was an open flat field about 100 yards deep and about 75 yards wide. It was here that I figured the Germans would defend if they intended a defense of the bridge." Dolan's intuition would prove out. A machine-gun opened up, halting the advance.

"I directed Lt. Donald Coxon to send his scouts out. This he did. He also went out with them. He had plenty of personal courage but he didn't have the heart to order them out without leading them. First Lieutenant Coxon was a seasoned combat officer and well-liked by his men as he was a leader." He said to Dolan ".. well sir, if I have to send someone out into that I'll go myself." Coxon took two scouts with him, and leading the way, crawled forward along the hedge. Dolan continues, "They got about 100 yards. A bullet killed one scout. Another bullet wounded Ferguson and Coxon. He was hit badly and started to come back. While he was moving along another bullet hit him in the stomach. After that, he bled to death. Second Lt. Robert E. McLaughlin took over the platoon. His radio operator, Corporal Frank Busa, moved forward and was hit by a sniper's bullet. McLaughlin thought Busa was alive and went out to get him but before McLaughlin could make it, he himself was hit in the upper leg, the one bullet went up through the lower part of his stomach and came out of his buttocks. I (Dolan) spotted the sniper and killed him. I then crawled to McLaughlin to give him first aid and carry him out. The lieutenant was in such excruciating pain he pleaded not to be moved. Later on, I went to get a cover for him as it started to rain that morning". When Dolan returned to cover McLaughlin, the wounded soldier was dead. By 0800 the action around the Manoir was getting intense. It was the full-fledged beginning of the four-day continuous, vicious battle, likely the worst killing ground in the Normandy airborne battle zones."

Lieutenant Dolan, Major McGinity and everybody in the area immediately returned fire for a few minutes. After leaving a few men at the spot to return some frontal fire, they took the platoon and flanked to the left to come up on one side of a hidden machine-gun nest.

At the same time, Dolan directed First Lieutenant George Wayne Presnell, the second platoon leader and a Sicily-tough combat officer, to head off and re-cross the road and get down to the river so that his platoon could approach the Manoir from the north side. Presnell and his men met no resistance until they moved along the dirt road which runs along the north hill side leading down to the Merderet and flooded prairie and across the street from the Manoir. Dolan wanted Presnell to envelop the Manoir, and coming from the north side, attack the Germans near the bridge.

The men momentarily gazed across the north and saw the great number of parachutes laying on top of the grassy waters. The thought that they were lucky they landed on dry ground passed through the minds of these 505 troopers. However, they also reasoned and suspected that if that many parachutes were in the marsh (the first time they even knew it was a flood plain) it was obvious the 507 or 508 Regiments may not be where they were supposed to have landed. This was a correct assumption because neither the 507 or 508 landed in the right place.

Meanwhile, the 1st Battalion in the midst of a desperate fight. The Germans encountered by the troopers fought with extraordinary tenacity. Charles Burghduff[8], a German speaking trooper of "N" Company, called to a group of German soldiers at a roadside roadblock to surrender. Their answer came back promptly in the form of a hail of rifle grenades and machine-pistol fire. Burghduff decided to convince them to surrender one way or another, and led a charge that killed twenty-three of the enemy. The remainder, three forlorn soldiers, finally called out, *"Kamerad".* By seven in the morning the battalion had won and organized on its first objective, the railroad bridge at Chef-du-Pont.

While Lieutenant Presnell and his platoon were approaching via the north side of the Manoir, Major McGinity, Dolan and his troops cut back after flanking the machine-gun and moved toward the spot where it was assumed to be located. Major McGinity was in the lead, with Dolan about four paces behind and slightly to his right. There was a high and thick hedgerow to their left. As this group moved forward, the Germans (who obviously had them in plain sight as they approached) opened up on them with

23

rifle fire and at least two *Schmeiser* sub-machine guns, the infamous *burp guns*. Major McGinity was killed instantly, hit many times before he fell. Dolan cut loose with his Tommy-gun aiming at the point where he saw the hedgerow leaves fluttering. He jumped into a nearby foxhole on his left and continued to fire as the 3rd platoon was exposed to enemy fire. They had Dolan pinned down but with him in that position the Krauts were not going forward.

At the same time enemy machine-gun and enemy rifle fire was steadily increasing from hidden hedgerow positions and firing at the "A" Company men trying to circle the Manoir. It was not possible to direct mortar fire, as no one knew where his buddies were located. Sergeant Prentiss Murray managed to drop a few 60mm mortar rounds on suspected machine-gun positions. However, continuous mortar fire was no longer feasible due to the proximity of our men.

While "A" Company was in dire straits, Colonel Ray Lindquist, commanding officer of the 508 PIR, could hear the rapid fire from where he had gathered with a group of 508 paratroopers. They were located 800 yards east of the Manoir and la Fiére bridge at the railroad crossing. He and his group moved forward to the south of the enemy fire. About 100 yards from where Dolan was under fire, Lindquist stopped and decided to move way to the left, in a southerly direction, and flank the enemy. His men could creep up the river-bank and attack to the north. Unbeknownst to anyone in "A" Company and the rest of the 505 First Battalion (after they left the drop zone and just as the machine pistol opened up on Major McGinity and Lieutenant Dolan's men), a group of about 45 men—mainly from the 507—had collected that morning on the east shore of the Merderet just north of the la Fiére causeway. Captain F.V. Schwarzwalder (later to gain prominence as the Head Coach of the 1959 National Championship Syracuse University football team) had assembled them on the east-side railway tracks. Possibly an hour before Gavin came across the marsh with 300 men from the 508 and about 45 men of the 507, the Schwarzwalder party began to advance against the closest known objective; the la Fiére bridge. This was done in order to get over the Merderet River to Schwarzwalder's target— Amfreville. They'd moved only a little distance along the southern side of the "Y" formed by the two roads when they were brought under fire by a German heavy machine-gun.

This was one of the enemy guns that had stopped Dolan and his men. Lieutenant John W. Marr, who was leading the point about 150 yards in advance of the 507 Company, looked back and saw that the Company had stopped. He decided to try to take the gun out by moving far over to the left, to come at the Manoir from the south, way over to the left side of the farm buildings. His group got down to the first hedgerow next to the river when gunfire broke out around them from a number of positions in and around the high stone buildings at the Manoir. Lieutenant Marr decided that the spot was too hot and he led his point scouts back to the company. As he withdrew, the German gun also opened up on Schwarzwalder and his 507 men. He ordered them to fire at the buildings and hedgerow. The enemy gun withdrew but was suppressed only for a moment. They killed only one enemy sniper. During this solitary skirmish it seemed to Marr, as he watched and listened, that some of the enemy fire was being directed toward the opposite flank. He had no way of knowing that this was because Company "A" 505 was attacking from the other side and behind the Manoir buildings.

"A" Company knew nothing about them either. Schwarzwalder told Marr to take his men and attempt to move forward along the hedgerow and get to a stone wall flanking the farm road which led over the bridge. Marr started across the field with four men. Two of them were shot through the legs by a machine-gun firing at 10-yards range as they closed on the hedgerow. They went down. T5 Escobar, one of the wounded men, opened fire on the German gun with his Tommy-gun, firing wildly. A German soldier rose out of the position with his arm cocked to heave a potato masher (grenade). Corporal Lawton holed him with his carbine. The German didn't die and stood there, still struggling to get the grenade off. Lawton and Private Parletto threw grenades together that blew up the machine-gun position and two Germans with it. By this time machine-pistol fire was raising hell against the hedgerow where the five point men lay. Corporal Lawton, who was bleeding badly from two wounds, spotted and shot a German officer who was casually looking at the action through binoculars from behind the bridge on the causeway. As Lawton was losing too much blood, Marr carried him several hedgerows back to the company with the rest of his four point men following.

Lieutenant Marr went back to confer with Captain Schwarzwalder about approaching from the flank. At this point Colonel Lindquist arrived on the scene with a large group of 508 men (actually led by Lieutenant John H. Wisner, the 2/507 G-2 officer). They all got off the road. At the same time, men of Company "C" 505 commanded by Captain Arthur Stefanich arrived by the lower road and met Presnell for a briefing. Being the senior officer, "Stef" took a few men to nail the enemy machine-gun, the one pestering Dolan and his men. Though he nearly got killed, Stefanich met with Dolan who in turn said he would take it out. Dolan made the decision to flank the Manoir on both the north and south sides.

Incredibly, this Marr 507 group was oblivious to the combat action that had been going on over on the right flank involving Company "A" 505. They knew nothing at all about it.

The Germans holed up in the massive solid stone Manoir homestead and farm buildings practically had a built-in fortress with small battlement-type rear windows. This enabled them to control a field of fire with little possibility of successful retaliation by small arms fire. The foot-thick side walls could not be penetrated. The large long retaining wall just off the south side by the bridge as well as the thick trees were natural spots for the German defense. They used it well until much later that morning when a squad of 508 men eventually got in behind the Manoir by killing the Germans who were firing out of the windows and the barnyard to the rear and left (south) side of the road.

While Dolan was pinned down and waiting for a possible enemy advance on his position he could hear continuous rifle and machine-gun firing down by the bridge on the north side. Dolan had heard Lieutenant Presnell with his men on the lower road next to the Manoir at the river's edge along with back up men on the side of the hill shooting down into the Manoir and barn building. The German defenders had automatic weapons. Riflemen traded round for round. Just before this skirmish started, Presnell and Private Harold J. Paul approached the bridge. While inspecting it, Presnell was shot at by scattered rifle fire. It hit his canteen only. The men promptly returned fire.

Staff Sergeant John Jampa, Jr., the A/505 second platoon ranking sergeant, got a patrol to go down the hill just above the Manoir to check out the enemy gunfire on the right side of the road. Squad Sergeant Ralph W. Barr led this patrol of four men, including Privates Charles F. Wernicks, James J. Currin (also pathfinder) and Harold Paul. They had only gone several yards from their now exposed position when a machine-gun opened up, killing all the men except Harold Paul who was pinned down and exposed. Nearby, Private George L. Bean and W. Stevenson were in a fire-fight with a big German. They threw a Gammon (high explosive) grenade at the German and killed him. At this point Lieutenant Presnell got his platoon back to a less exposed position and read-ied them for another attack.

Lieutenant Oakley, Corporal Oscar L. Queen and their first platoon patrol had gone down the hedgerows and hill to the left of the Manoir and reached the river edge on the south side. They never saw or encountered the 507 men who were further to the south and more distant. Hedgerows lay between these two forces.

The "A" Company men were nearly on top of the Germans when they were fired on by machine and burp guns. Lieutenant Oakley and Oscar Queen killed three defenders. They ran around the river's edge and barn building to the stone wall near the road-way and bridge. They spotted a machine-gun firing out of the Manoir into Presnell's men. As Queen ran forward to knock out that machine-gunner, a potato masher grenade exploded a few feet away from him. The force of the explosion knocked him down, stunning him slightly. Oscar Queen was a fine combat soldier, a Texan who was as skilled at breaking in steer as killing the en-emy. While Queen was laying there he heard a .45 pistol in rapid-fire, fire directly behind him. He spotted a German in a tree just above him and took this sniper out with his carbine. He then ran back across the Manoir, got behind the wall and called for his machine-gun. He talked to Captain Dale A. Roysdon, the Regi-mental G3. Roysdon had fired his .45 pistol at the German who threw the grenade at Queen, not the sniper in the tree. The Cap-tain had seen the soldier throwing the grenade at Queen from the nearby south side barn building area which was out of Queen's view.

After Oscar Queen had gotten his .30 caliber light machine-gun set up and firing, they eliminated the Germans on the right side entrance way to the Manoir and gained a direct field of fire from behind the stone wall at and into the Manoir property. "A"

Company now had control of the north side and yard of the Manoir as well as the little bridge running over the causeway westerly to the hamlet of Cauquigny, across the enormous flood plain. The 508 would take the Manoir (south side) backyard within ten minutes.

At (about) 0900 hours, while "A" Company was making their costly approach, working down both sides of the line towards the Manoir along the east bank of the river, the First Battalion (505) commander Major Frederick C.A. Kellam had just been approached by Brigadier General Jim Gavin. The young, 38 year old general was leading a cohort of 300 men (mainly from the 507) who were totally mis-dropped and had assembled a mile away. He could hear the noise of the 505 "A" Company fire-fight as he traveled down the railroad to the sound of the guns with his soaking wet paratroopers who had just crossed over the marsh from the shore. Kellam told General Gavin that he had everything under control and there should be no problem taking the Manoir building after a cautious approach. No enemy had tried to come over the bridge from the west so Gavin was satisfied with Kellam's report and assurances. He, as the former colonel and original 505 commander, (July 6, 1942) had absolute faith and confidence in his 505 officers and paratroopers. They had proven themselves competent and aggressive soldiers in Sicily and Italy and he knew they would prove themselves again at the bridge.

With satisfaction that Major Kellam had his First Battalion mission solidly under control, Gavin took off for the Chef-du-Pont bridge along with Lieutenant Colonel Arthur A. Maloney (507) (another red head) and Lieutenant Colonel Edwin J. Ostberg (507). Both Maloney and Ostberg were battalion commanders *sans* their battalions. Gavin took them and their men to seize and defend the Chef-du-Pont bridge and possibly occupy, or at least scout, Hill 30 which was part of the 508 PIR original mission, as well as defend the surrounding area. It did not take this brilliant combat general long to determine that the 508 had also been scattered and was not at regimental strength. The battle at Chef-du-Pont that ensued later in the afternoon with Lieutenant Colonel Ostberg, and his pick-up group of about 150 paratroopers, (and that evening with Captain Creek) will be reported on later.

By the time Lieutenant John Dolan was ready to make his final attack, Colonel Lindquist was in a field near the bend in the road 300 yards above the Manoir. He sent word to Dolan that his (Lindquist's) men would attack from the left/south-side while "A" Company attacked from the right side. Dolan not only never received Lindquist's message, he had not seen nor heard from Lindquist all morning. At about 0900, after General Gavin had talked to Major Kellam, he told Colonel Lindquist to set up a reserve force by the railroad crossing and to take what he had of Company "B"—508 men—and move forward as a supporting force for A/505. After Presnell, Corporal Oscar Queen and the first and second platoons of "A" Company had cleared the Manoir roadside yard and entrance on the north side in front of the bridge, a group of 508 Paratroopers came from around the last farm barn building to the rear on the southeast side. They attacked along the pathway between that barn and the fort-like Manoir homestead. This 508 group included First Sergeant Ralph Thomas, Sergeant Jim Blue and Lieutenant Hagar A/508 and other enlisted men who were about to add the finishing touch to the fight for the Manoir.

First Sergeant Thomas of E /508 had landed off course hours before near the 505 DZ. He later met Colonel Lindquist. They assembled at the nearby east railroad crossing, as did 600 other 507 and 508 scattered troopers. By the time the A/505 attack was well in progress on the right, Sergeant Thomas took off with his E/508 mixed group on Lindquist's order. Another group under command of A/508 Lieutenant Hagar, along with Sergeant James Blue and Robert J. Broderick F/508, were in on this Manoir 'clean-up' crew. They heard the shooting stop from the northeast end of the farm house and they began entering into the backyard. There were dead Germans observed in the yard by Sergeant Thomas as they cautiously moved ahead. At the same time, Lieutenant Dolan and Colonel Ekman (505 CO) were casually standing in the driveway talking over the situation (as the Manoir battle was over as far as they were concerned) when shooting started in the backyard. Some ten or twelve Germans started firing out of the second floor windows of the M. Louis Leroux's Manoir homestead. Everyone in the 508 patrol returned fire.. After ten minutes one of the Germans waived a white flag out the window. The Lieutenant told Sergeant Jim Blue to go up and tell the Krauts to come out *Hande Hoch*—hands up. While Blue was telling the Lieutenant it was a better idea to have all the Germans come out of the building, a young trooper went forward with rifle in hand to accept the surrender. He was shot dead. The German probably didn't know the white flag was being waved out another window. After more shooting and Sergeant Palmer emptying his Tommy-gun up through the upstairs floor boards, the final surrender took effect that ended the battle for the Leroux Manoir. A bazooka round from A/505 into the Manoir had helped speed that decision.

First sergeant Ralph Thomas spoke to the farmer Louis Leroux who had been holed up in the wine cellar during the entire battle along with his wife and three children. The family took off that day to visit another farmer friend, which was indeed fortunate because a battle *royale* that would rage non-stop for three more days and nights would soon begin. He wouldn't recognize his homestead when he returned. Nearly half of the front of the rugged stone family home would be blown away in the ensuing battle.

After the last round had been fired in the Manoir skirmish the critical defense positions were set up by Colonel Lindquist and Major Kellam. As it was the specific mission of Kellam's 505 First Battalion to seize the la Fiére Bridge and, Lindquist was ordered by General Gavin to go back and set up a solid reserve defense force. It was Kellam's men of the First Battalion 505 who were now holding tight on the easterly edge of the la Fiére bridge. "A" Company was on both the left and right sides with two bazookas on each side of the bridge. All available land mines were put on the west side end of the bridge. A disabled German ammunition carrier open truck that was parked on the edge of the Manoir property was rolled onto the bridge by Presnell and a gang of A/505 troopers.

Last but not least, a 57mm anti-tank cannon had been brought to the Manoir area about 0830 hours by Lieutenant David W. Connally Jr., Finlayson, Robert E. Klein and most of the men from the third platoon of Company B-307 Parachute Engineer Battalion. They worked all night and in the early daylight to salvage that precious 57mm gun out of a wrecked glider. B/307 Para-Engineers were a solid part of the 505 Regimental Combat Team and were assigned to Kellam to ensure the la Fiére Bridge would not be blown up in case it was rigged with German explosives. That 57mm gun would figure heavily in the battle that afternoon but could not be used in the ongoing early morning attack to assist in the capture of the Manoir. As B/505 was without any officer, Major Kellam put B/307 Engineer Lieutenant David Connally in command of a small group of Company B/505 troopers that were down in the bridge area. Later that afternoon a B/505 officer arrived and took over from Connally.

Forty two 80th AAA gliders landed in or near the 505 Drop Zone "O" at 0400 hours along with ten other gliders. By mid morning on D-Day these artillery-men had four 57mm cannons set up with five good jeeps. By noon a fifth gun had been recovered. By 1730 hours on D-Day Captain Norman G. Nelson's overlay showed 6 guns in position and in operation. At least one 57mm cannon was located directly at the bend of the road on the east side, just above the la Fiére Bridge. That gun was vital to its defense against the 3 German tanks later eliminated by the "A" Company bazooka teams. Their cannon figured into the battle the next day although it would run into bad luck with two direct hits through its shield.

NOTES FOR CHAPTER 3:

6. John Dolan commanded "A" Company through Normandy and part of the way through Holland until severe wounds caused long hospitalization and eventually, retirement. He practiced law in Boston and was a good friend of the author (a trial lawyer in Boston for 40+ years and still at it in 1999).

7. Captain Dolan wrote a seven page letter to General Gavin on March 23, 1959 highlighting his and the "A" Company seizure of the bridge. An exact copy of the letter is found in the Appendix of this documentary. Not being a egotist, he stated only the bare essentials. In his P.S. he noted that ".. for the record, this bridge was held by Company "A" from the time of its capture on "D" Day, until we were relieved."

8. Charles Burghduff a fellow pathfinder and sergeant. He was killed in action next to me, during an attack on the town of Mook, Holland on September 19, 1944. Charley Burghduff was a good friend, intelligent and brave and we shared German parentage (my mother's mom and dad were immigrants from Germany, via Basel, Switzerland).

Chapter 4
ACROSS THE CAUSEWAY

With the First Battalion 505 mission accomplished at a dear expense to A/505 and the 507 and 508 troopers, it was with determination that Captain F. V. 'Ben' Schwarzwalder and his group of 507 men would gain that 750 yard la Fiére causeway and join their 507 Regiment if possible.

As he did previously on going to the south side of the Manoir (and knocking off a sniper), Lieutenant John Marr again led the pack. This time he was joined by lead scout Private James L. Mattingly, starting across the causeway at about 1345 hours. A captured NCO prisoner had told Marr there were German infantrymen dug-in and strung-out along the causeway. They were apparently trapped between the east and west sides of the bridgehead as, unbeknownst to Marr, a group of 507 men were already dug in at the old Cauquigny church wall. Private Mattingly, being so forewarned, was quick to empty his M1 into the foxhole of a German who had jumped up and fired at him. Mattingly also went flat and threw a grenade into the hole, killing one and wounding another enemy soldier. A total of seven Germans then rose out of their holes to surrender to him. He pointed his empty gun at them to move back east. He was covered by his backup point-man, Private Jonnie K. Ward.

After clearing the enemy and walking along the causeway they spotted two German MG-42 machine-guns that could have mowed down the entire group. Obviously, these high-powered guns were the ones firing early on in the Manoir battle and later along the tree-lined causeway. While reveling in their accomplishment one of Marr's men was shot in the buttocks by a sniper firing from the southwest side of the causeway. On nearing the end they broke out an orange flag as they thought they spotted Americans. Sure enough, they saw an orange smoke flare near the Cauquigny church. It was first Lieutenant Lewis Levy of D/507 along with second Lieutenant Joseph Kormylo both of Company D 507 PIR along with some 508 troopers.

This group of fifty 507 and 508 men that landed on the western end of the causeway had set up a defense position around the perimeter of the Cauquigny church with one bazooka. Lieutenant Colonel Charles J. Timmes' 507 was pinned down and stuck in an orchard with his men (for four days) but could get a runner in and out from time to time. Early on D-Day Timmes ordered Levy to stay at the church to guard that spot against an attack from the west and to protect his southern defense line. Everything went along fine that morning and Levy even had a happy farmer bring his men milk and cider to wash down their K-rations. The only problem this group had was getting shot at by the troopers on the east bank rather than by the Germans on the causeway, but no one was hurt. Lieutenant Levy gave Captain Schwarzwalder and Lieutenant Marr a report on all the positions he was familiar with on his west side of the Merderet River including Timmes' now dangerous orchard location about a mile northwest of the causeway on the edge at the marsh. After that briefing Lieutenant Levy walked across the causeway to the Manoir and spoke with Colonel Lindquist. Lindquist immediately packed up and started to gather his 508 men in order to move to the west side of the causeway where they were supposed to have landed in the first place.

Before Lindquist arrived, Schwarzwalder decided to go to the aid of Timmes' trapped group, north of Cauquigny. He took off with all his men, hoping to eventually attack Amfreville and possibly locate Colonel George V. Millet Jr., the 507 Regimental commander (who was captured by the Germans). When he left to look for Timmes he was joined by all the 508 men with the exception of two officers and eight enlisted men who stayed at the church; certainly too few to defend the west side bridgehead. The other 508 men going over the causeway were accompanied by Private First Class Francis Buck (505) on orders from Major

Kellam to return with any 505 men to the Manoir defensive position. It was a good time for the stragglers of all regiments to locate and join their units. While looking for 505 troopers PFC Buck walked beyond the church when he heard the unmistakable clank of tanks coming from the west along with distant but approaching machine-gun fire. As a combat veteran, he knew what these sounds meant.

As Buck hurried past the Cauquigny church he saw a 507 officer and warned him and his men of approaching enemy tanks. The officer told Buck that the tanks were not his problem and somebody else would take care of them. Buck, though outranked, was a prudent combat soldier who would not respond to this seemingly inexperienced officer. However, it wasn't long before this small group engaged the enemy and then high-tailed it across the causeway. It would not be crossed again for three days.

When Major Kellam got the word on Buck's rapid return he immediately relayed the tank report to Dolan and all other officers and sergeants in command around the bridge. "Dig in, deeper, and get ready." "A" Company lined up and spread out on the east side of the causeway. They already had some land mines and the disabled German ammo truck sitting in the middle of the bridge as preparations against enemy attack.

Additional separate groups from "C" company 505 led by First Lieutenant Jack Tallerday and Sergeant Sylvester Meis had arrived earlier. Tallerday took command of C/505 as Captain Stefanich had been wounded earlier by a sniper. The balance of B/505 was present with one of its regular officers. The most powerful, yet rather inadequate defense weapons they had was a 57mm antitank gun on the corner of the road 300 yards up hill from the bridge and Manoir by the 80th Airborne Antiaircraft Battalion glidermen. Also, by the side of the bridge were four of the toughest bazooka-team men in Ste. Mere Eglise; namely Private First Class Lenold Peterson, the gunner, to the left of the bridge with his assistant, Private Marcus Heim, Jr. and PFC John D. Bolderson, the gunner, with his assistant, loader Private Gordon C. Pryne. They were backed up by the heavy weapons Headquarters Company First Battalion 505 with machine-guns placed in strategic positions. Lieutenant John Otto, a fine soldier, was in charge of the Headquarters weapons men.

The only way the German tanks were going to get through to

Ste. Mere Eglise or Utah Beach was over the causeway and the little la Fiére Bridge. The First Battalion felt confident they could stop the enemy combined-arms attack if they had artillery support and adequate ammunition. The mortar, machine-gun and rifle ammunition was being brought to the Manoir by Private Richard Reyes A/505 who was hauling ammo back and forth from para-bundles down to the Manoir. That afternoon, this First Battalion group of seasoned paratroopers had no idea if seaborne forces had even landed at Utah Beach, seven miles to the east. Neither did Generals Ridgway or Gavin have the slightest idea if the 4th Division had arrived The 4th Division did successfully land at 0630 hours but they were nowhere near the la Fiére bridge this day and were of little or no help that day or the next.

Across the now enemy-cleared causeway and near the Cauquigny church, Lieutenants Lewis Levy and Kormylo could hear the tanks as they walked west and ahead 200 yards to get a look and a one time shot at them. A buck private, whose name was unknown to either Lieutenant, was with Kormylo. On seeing the top of the tank turrets and enemy riflemen across the way, the two of them threw grenades and opened up with their rifles before running back beyond where Levy was covering them. As they ran past Levy he yelled for them to keep on going while he watched the Germans move in and set up a machine-gun. He threw a grenade and disposed of the gun crew with his rifle.

Captain Schwarzwalder, who was determined to seize his D-Day mission, had left Levy and led his 80-man group of 507 troopers along the marsh, to the north in search of Timmes. They made it to the orchard 1000 yards from the church and settled in with Timmes and his group from the Second Battalion of the 507. This force numbered about 120 men. It was indeed unfortunate because they became isolated in this orchard for the next three days; until 9 June. Meanwhile, back at the Cauquigny church, a mini-war was going on as a handful of courageous troopers determined to face the enemy on their own. They had no bazookas, only a machine-gun and M1 rifles or their carbines. They waited for the 1057th Grenadier Regiment, along with its supporting armor from the 100th Panzer Replacement Battalion of the German 91st Division.

At about 1600 hours a few rounds of German artillery or mortars landed on the causeway in front of the church. The tanks where shelling the church with the infantry closing up on the side of the road next to it. Both sides were now about ten yards apart throwing grenades at one another. Private Orlin Stewart was on the west side of the church at the fork in the road when he saw a bazooka round hit a tank. Then two other Renault tanks tried to get past the damaged tank while a volley of rifle fire erupted along the enemy line. To Stewart's surprise, a First Sergeant and Private who were total strangers to him, began a three-man battle with the enemy. This mystery Sergeant and Private had a handful of Gammon grenades they both threw against the tanks while Stewart covered them with his Browning Automatic Rifle (BAR). They disabled both tanks and the unknown Sergeant killed the crews with a fragmentation grenade as they tried to bail out. As a medium tank moved up from behind Stewart, his buddies discovered they were out of grenades and ammunition and decided they had only seconds to disappear behind the hedgerows. Levy, Kormylo and other six men got out in a hurry and joined Timmes at the orchard defense zone, entering from along the waterside marsh. They were safe for the moment (Levy was later killed in action).

The problem now was with Company B 508 PIR who were partly across the causeway. Some of them had turned left (south) at the Cauquigny church road intersection. When mortars and artillery hit your area, you go to ground or hit the road, fast. While the Levy and Stewart band were doing their job with grenades behind the hedgerows, the Germans broke out of their hidden positions and poured into the area firing with automatic weapons and light mortars. B/508 was caught wide open and could not get back along the causeway. They were overwhelmed with firepower and most of the survivors went into the marsh seeking the protection of the tall reeds while wading or swimming through the flood plain back toward the Manoir east side. Many men were killed or died of their wounds while in the marsh. Observing from the Manoir on the east bank, we could clearly see them in the marsh as well as the German tanks and infantry over on the western shore. Colonel Lindquist had just walked back from his briefing on the west side of the Cauquigny bridgehead in order to set up this 508 Regimental Command Post (CP) which had not been done due to the fast moving battle for the Manoir de la Fiére during the morning.

Just before the west bank attack had begun at 1700 hours, Lieutenant Dolan's Company "A" had wasted no time digging deep foxholes and setting up defensive positions following to Francis Buck's tank alert. Sporadic artillery and mortar rounds continued to come in. The First Battalion 505 men on the east side of the Merderet did not heed the 507 and 508 men crossing over the causeway earlier that afternoon but almost everyone who looked up could see, especially on the south-side, the poor souls trying to escape death while wading through the marsh. It was impossible for the 1/505 to come to the aid of these B/508 men and F/508 troopers as their guns could not reach the far shore with any accuracy. Their bullets were of no use against enemy tanks. Only the 57mm at the bend of the road was shooting back with any effect. Sgt. Joe Harald, Corporal Glen Bell Pvt. Vaught of F/508 made it back to the east river-bank but a Lieutenant was killed according to Bob Broderick of F/508 who was on the east bank.

The Germans soon gave up the hunt against the men in the marsh and their Renault tanks started to roll very slowly out onto the causeway. Just then, German artillery and mortars took the offensive and poured fire around the Manoir, with shrapnel bursting with a lethal radius of 100 yards in each direction. Tree-height shell-bursts, which are horrific because the exploding shrapnel can get right down into your hole (whereas ordinary rounds hitting the ground outside your dugout spreads its shrapnel up and outward and not directly on top of you), were coming down among the defenders..

la Fiére Bridge Defense 1600H 6 June

After that extremely heavy artillery bombardment the Germans became very aggressive and at 1600 hours three tanks moved forward very slowly along the causeway. The panzers were followed by approximately 200 infantrymen, many of whom were intermingled with and between their supporting armor. The enemy lifted his artillery fire as his tanks and men approached our position. After the enemy barrage lifted, the men of First Battalion 505 fired their small arms and machine-guns at the attacking German infantry. The first tank rolled within forty yards of the la Fiére bridge, apparently spotting the mines out in front of the disabled German flat-bed truck. The tank hatch opened and

37

the commander stood up for a quick look. That was the last look he ever had.

A bazooka team from either "B" or "C" Company was also on the south shore. Three hours before the tank attack, a 57mm cannon arrived and Dolan put it at the bend of the roadway above the Manoir. He positioned Elijah Starr and Harold Rose with a .30 caliber machine-gun right next to the 57mm gun. The cannon fired at the tanks until it ran out of ammunition. This 57mm gun had a direct view down the hill but its view was partly obscured by the top of the truck on the bridge. The Germans also had a direct view of our gunners operating the cannon. Private Clarence Becker, on the left flank, fired his machine-gun at the exposed German tank commander. Every other riflemen took advantage of this stupid blunder and opened up on him and the infantry also. The bazooka-men held their fire until that moment because the tree foliage at the bend of the causeway kept them from getting a clear view of the oncoming column.

The first two tanks were some 15 or 20 yards from each other with the third tank 50 yards to their rear. When the lead tank approached to within forty yards of the bridge the two "A" Company bazooka teams manned by Private First Class Lenold Peterson with assistant gunner Private Marcus Heim, Jr. on the left and Private First Class John D. Bolderson with his assistant Gordon C. Pryne on the right, got up and fired rockets from the edge of the road. They were under the heaviest small arms fire from the other side of the causeway as well as from cannon and machine-gun fire from the tanks. Nevertheless, their bazooka fire had a training-camp calm and accuracy about it. After being hit, the lead tank fired its cannon at the Peterson/Heim team and snapped a concrete pole in front of them, sending flying chunks of concrete in the air. Peterson now ran 20 feet to get an unobstructed shot at the tanks with Heim beside him carrying a bag of extra rockets.

To this day, I cannot understand why all four of them were not killed. They fired and reloaded with the precision of well-oiled machinery. I don't think that either team wasted a shot. The first tank received several direct hits. A tread was knocked off and within a matter of minutes it was on fire. This tank tried to get off the causeway by going to its left while the second tank tried to get around it. During all this bazooka action, our 57mm gun was firing from up on the hill and the tanks were returning fire on it.

The bazooka-teams soon went to work on the second tank. Within 30 seconds it too was on fire. Peterson put another round into the tank's turret as it swung around to take a pot shot at him. As Peterson was running out of rockets he sent Marcus Heim over the other side of the bridge to get extra ammunition. Heim ran through a hail of enemy bullets only to find the Bolderson bazooka with a hole blown through it. He picked up a bag of rockets he found and ran back to Peterson's side. They then hit the second tank seven more times. As the panzer crew tried to back away, their tank burst into flames, incinerating the crew. After firing every rocket they had, Peterson and Heim jumped into the cover of their foxholes. In the meantime, the 57mm continued firing and eventually knocked out the last tank. All four men of the bazooka teams were awarded the Distinguished Service Cross for this action.

Captain Arthur M. Stefanich and Lieutenant Gerald N. Johnson, both of Company C 505, (Sicily and Italy combat veterans) along with seventy men who dropped some distance northeast of the 505 DZ picked up their para-bundles and made a forced march directly for the la Fiére bridge, their assigned D-Day mission. They spread out and got in a quick lick against the enemy that morning by destroying a German armored truck with a Gammon grenade. They also took two prisoners along the way. When they reached the bend in the road near the la Fiére Bridge they heard the pitched battle and machine-gun fire from several different directions. Stefanich went off to find Battalion Headquarters or anyone in command. He returned about an hour later and said Major McGinity had been killed and that they better move forward. At the bend of the road where John Dolan had set up the 57mm gun they crossed over and were immediately fired upon They escaped into a deep roadside ditch along the hedgerow. Johnson yelled to 'Stef' that he was on fire and the Captain jumped on top of him to put out the flames. A bullet had pierced a smoke bomb in Stefanich's pocket, wounding him. Johnson had to toss his smoke bomb in the roadway as a screen to get his company commander back to C/505 troops and a medic.

Upon returning to the la Fiére upper roadway near the 57mm gun, Lieutenant Johnson noticed there was no men manning the gun. He thought that odd as he didn't see any dead gunners or men near it. He dashed over to it. He had previous artillery school training and knew he could fire the weapon if there were shells nearby. Upon examination of the cannon, he found the firing pin missing, standard procedure by artillery-men if a gun is abandoned. It was obvious that this gun had been in use and fired. There were no 57mm shells around it. The gun was now useless but it would do great service the next day (on D+2). Johnson and his C/505 men fought on the top of the hill and placed a lot of 60mm mortar and machine-gun fire down on the causeway. They also protected the "A" Company flanks from any infiltration attack which might come from the north or south side of the bridge.

When the two bazooka-teams called for more ammunition, Major Kellam, Captain Roysdon and Frank Buck went hunting for extra rockets. While they were gathering ammunition the Germans opened up with more mortar fire on the whole perimeter. Major Kellam was killed and Captain Roysdon was severely wounded and rendered unconscious from the concussion. Lieutenant Dolan took over command of the First Battalion as he was the senior officer present. Dolan and a Lieutenant Weir (Regt. HQ.) carried Roysdon back to an aid station but he died late that evening. Francis Buck stayed on until ordered out with shrapnel wounds.

During the close-up fight at the bridge, the men of Company "A" in the main line of fire along the embankment had concentrated on the large group of German infantry which had come along behind the tanks. From their dug-in positions the paratrooper's guns were able to put a grazing fire on the bridge and causeway. The result was like mowing hay. The leading files of enemy soldiers fell in their tracks along the causeway embankment. Those Germans still beyond the bend in the causeway managed to retreat west to the vicinity of the Cauquigny church. The infantry did not attempt to force the la Fiére Bridge crossing again during the evening or the night of D-Day. The first battle for this bridge was won by our men, but at a great cost. And the Germans still owned the west side of the "bridgehead".

Company "B" 505 PIR was put into reserve in the perimeter of Company "A" so that we had an almost 360° degree defense-line. The rest of the evening we spent under heavy mortar and machine-gun fire. The mortar fire was very effective against the two forward platoons because of tree bursts. It took very little imagination on the part of the Germans to figure out just where we would be dug-in. As Dolan later recalled, "there was less than a seventy five yard frontage on either side of the bridge from where we could effectively defend. Accordingly, they could throw their mortar fire in our general direction with good results. During the night the fire let up slightly but they started early the next morning and kept it up." Dolan's third platoon took the worst beating, as they were in a heavily wooded area.

General Gavin was on a reconnaissance mission to Chef-du-Pont with Lieutenant Colonels Maloney and Ostberg along with Gavin's aide Captain Olson. The bitter fight in that area had not started by mid afternoon so Gavin left Ostberg and his 507 men to attack the bridge and the Chef-du-Pont causeway as Maloney saw fit. Gavin returned to the la Fiére Bridge late in the evening and after the battle, to find almost all the officers dead or badly wounded and the senior ranking officer in command of the First Battalion, namely, First Lieutenant John J. Dolan. Gavin sent for Lieutenant Colonel Mark Alexander, a very courageous combat leader, to take over command of the First Battalion. General Gavin was of the correct opinion that the Germans would not mount another attack that night and the Final Battalion men were now secure in defensive positions backed up by Colonel Lindquist's 508 force at the rear railroad embankment. All the American dead and wounded were being carried out under darkness with assistance of stretchers and jeeps beyond the bend of the road. While enemy artillery and rifle fire was peppering the area, Private First Class Thomas A. Bresch, a company clerk, volunteered to remove the seriously wounded in a jeep he recovered from a glider. He drove it to the spot hidden by the easterly bend in the road above the Manoir and he heroically evacuated 18 men during the battle. The field at the road bend was the first aid station administered by a medical orderly and hero, Private Kelly W. Byars of A/505. The field was also the holding spot for our men killed in action. The most seriously wounded men who needed immediate attention were the first to be transported out by the jeep to the Battalion or Regimental doctors and senior Sergeant Fred Morgan.

General Gavin went back to the railroad crossing and set up his "Force A" command post for the night. Unfortunately for him, a messenger woke him and said General Ridgway wanted to see him. Gavin and his aide walked in moonlight back to the Division CP, outside Ste. Mere Eglise, and found it was a wasted trip as Ridgway was asleep. After awakening the General, he passed on the message that everything was under control, and "just do what has to be done". No doubt some nervous staff officer wanted Brigadier Jim Gavin back at the Division CP and sent the message in Ridgway's name. The astonishing occurrence was that Gavin, and his aide Olson, while heading to see Ridgway, passed a German battalion moving between Ste. Mere Eglise and the la Fiére Bridge (probably heading to Neuville au Plain after the battle with Lieutenant Turner Turnbull's heroic D/505 platoon).

It may have been Gavin's battle-hardened sixth sense that led him to place most of Colonel Lindquist's 508 Battalion 800 yards to the rear of the Manoir at the railroad embankment that first afternoon. In any event, the choice was fortuitous. The 505 First Battalion, or what remained of it, could have been wiped out by another frontal attack across the causeway while simultaneously being hit from the rear if it was no so-positioned. One 82nd man, Captain Miller, (who spoke German) did run into the German infiltration group that General Gavin missed by so few yards. Miller was taken prisoner (he escaped two days later).

The 507 force of 121 men and 21 officers pinned down with Lieutenant Colonel Timmes' north of Cauquigny now included the Marr and Schwarzwalder group that arrived after crossing the causeway when the Manoir was captured. Their location, was in the "Orchard" about one mile northwest of the la Fiére bridge and 1100 yards from the Cauquigny bridgehead. The Germans knew there was a sunken road right behind the orchard, through the marsh, and over to the east side of the Merderet. They undoubtedly felt that Timmes' men were an advance party that would attack them, so they kept constant pressure on the orchard positions. Although this group of soldiers was never charged by the enemy, they were kept under constant rifle, mortar and machine-gun fire for the next two days. Thirty five of their numbers became battle casualties during that time. Although neither force attacked the other, they kept each other in check.

One can theorize that if Timmes' men were not defending that orchard perimeter the German 1057th Grenadiers could have crossed over the marsh on the northern sunken-road at night and attacked the 505 men dug in at la Fiére from the rear as well as the 508 troopers back at the railroad embankment. Although no one on either side knew it at the time, a better strategic location for Timmes' force couldn't have been planned. Once again luck, or the intuition of veteran small unit commanders, broke our way.

Chef Du Pont on D-Day - the 'other' bridge

After General Gavin arrived at Chef-du-Pont he and his group had a firefight about 1030 hours with a stopped armed train and its German guards. After repulsing this force, Gavin immediately went to find the other bridge running over the same Merderet River. He found the Chef-du-Pont Bridge and raised causeway over the flooded marsh one half mile outside of town, to the southwest. From there, Gavin could see Hill 30 over to his right about one mile away. It looked as if it was surrounded by the marsh (although it wasn't on the northwest side). During the original approach to Chef-du-Pont, Gavin and Maloney split up into two forces of about seventy-five men each, later meeting up at the bridge. General Gavin, Lieutenant Colonel Ostberg and their seventy-five 507 men went straight down the railroad tracks. A Frenchmen along the way said there were no Germans in Chef-du-Pont. He was wrong. There were roughly forty Germans in and around the houses but after a short skirmish the enemy took off for the causeway with the paratroopers in pursuit. General Gavin left Ostberg to seize the bridge at about 1100 hours (D-Day) as opposition seemed very light. However, outside of town the enemy had a solid defense line dug in at the Chef-du-Pont bridge and all along the causeway with machine-gun emplacements and riflemen in foxholes. Some fleeing Germans dove into their dugouts east of the bridge but most got across to the other side. Ostberg and his men stopped firing and waited a few minutes on the east side of the bridge. A German soldier got up out of his hole with his hands in the air and called "*Kamerad*". He was shot dead from 20 feet. Another minute passed and another German from the same dugout stood up with his hands in the air. He was also shot dead. While there was no excuse for our actions, the remaining Germans could now only do one thing: fight to the finish. And that they did because they could neither escape nor surrender.

The troopers then went ahead and picked off all the enemy on their (east) side of the bridge. As the bridge rose up from the road there was no way of seeing the enemy on the other side. However, the Germans on the causeway ramp apparently saw the paratroopers as they, in turn, were picked off if they raised their heads out of the dugouts formerly occupied by the Germans.

Ostberg and a small group of his men tried to rush the bridge with bursts of machine-gun and rifle fire. Ostberg was wounded in the charge but fortunately fell into the safety of the marsh. While the afternoon wore on with continuing grenade duels and pot shots traded, Lieutenant Colonel Maloney and all of his men (except 34 troopers) were ordered to get back to the la Fiére Manoir and bridge as quickly as possible. General Gavin was afraid that a massive attempt by German artillery and tanks may carry that bridge into enemy hands. He needed every man he could collect in case of a second charge at la Fiére.

With Ostberg out of action Captain Roy E. Creek C/507 took command of the remaining defenders. The Germans, with all their 91st Division armaments in place or on call, moved up a light cannon within 600 yards of our lines. Shell fire from this enemy infantry gun took out fourteen of our troopers. While the shelling and harassing from deadly rifle fire poured in on the 507 men, some of the troopers called out to Captain Creek to look to the rear. Creek saw a line of enemy infantry to the north of him deploying 300 yards away amid the outer village farm buildings. He had to deal with an attack from the rear as well as incoming artillery with an obvious attack coming at him from across the bridge to his front. Creek figured those Germans behind him must have hidden in the buildings and stayed there when the larger 507 Maloney-Ostberg force first arrived that morning and attacked the train and the village of Chef-du-Pont, bypassing them during the fight down to the bridge.

Like manna from heaven that evening (though it was still daylight) a glider landed intact at 2110 hours right in the middle of Creek's men. The glidermen from Battery "C" of 80th Airborne Anti-Aircraft Battalion brought forth a 57mm cannon which was quickly turned against the German gun, putting it out of action with two rounds. Meanwhile, more help arrived in the form of a Division staff officer, who earlier ran as fast as he could to get help for Ostberg and Creek, returning at the same time as the glider arrival with a platoon of troopers who systematically routed the 1057th Grenadier attacking infantry. The Germans ran and took positions all along the causeway in their dugouts. The 507 men, with their newly arrived backup force stayed on their side of the bridge. Roy Creek took a walk north along the Merderet River, now that it was getting dark, in hopes of finding a better defensive position. He found a spot where the lay of the land provided him a clear field of fire west across the marsh. His men jumped at this opportunity to redeploy to better firing positions. They could see every German in their foxholes and after ten minutes of weathering machine-gun fire across the marsh they killed or wounded all the enemy defenders except two soldiers who fled as fast as they could run.

Creek and his men moved across the Chef-du-Pont Bridge and settled in to defend it. It had taken the entire day to seize the crossing with the small force at hand. As this causeway was at least 700 yards distant to the other end they had a wide open shot at any tanks or infantry that might attack them that night or in the morning. There were 40 dead Germans in their holes or laid out on the embankment compared to 13 dead and 23 wounded Americans. The 507 PIR paratroopers succeeded in seizing the second bridge, one of the priority D-Day missions of the 82nd Airborne Division.

The 507 PIR was first into Chef-du-Pont and seized the east side of the bridge on D-Day. Clearly that honor belongs to the 507 men under Lieutenant Colonel Arthur Maloney of the 507 PIR along with Lieutenant Colonel Ostberg and Captain Roy Creek. There might have been a few 508 troopers that the Gavin force picked up along the way, but the 507 boys took Chef-du-Pont and held that little bridge over the Merderet all day and night of D-Day. In fact, there are two interesting stories about Chef-du-Pont. There's the one account of the men with Roy Creek being "saved by the bell" by the glider that floated in with the 57mm cannon (recounted above). The other incident concerns Maloney, who was a big 230 pound six-footer. He was fighting his way to the Chef-du-Pont Bridge on the afternoon of D-Day. Under cover of a white phosphorus grenade he got onto the bridge. A German threw a potato masher grenade at him. He turned and ran to get out of harm's way but the enemy grenade exploded and threw Maloney up into the air. While up in the air his legs were still running, causing the men to laugh at the "old man" running like hell in mid air.

On 7 June, Colonel Lindquist and his 508 force relieved Captain Creek and all his 507 men at about 1600 hours. The 508 men continued the Chef-du-Pont Bridge seizure and then began the attack mission across the causeway. They were successful by the night of 8 June. The 508 had forced the Germans across the Chef-du-Pont causeway.

The D-Day action was concluded with the 505 Parachute Infantry Regimental Combat Team securely dug in at their triangular positions in the Ste. Mere Eglise area. The First Battalion was dug in at the la Fiére Bridge after their fight for the Manoir and their man-versus-tank battle. Most of the battalion officers that were in this area were killed or so severely wounded to be out of action. "Red Dog" Dolan of A/505 was in command of the First Battalion until late in the day when Lieutenant Colonel Mark Alexander decided, along with Major John Norton, an S3, to get down to the Manoir, take command and hold that bridge at all costs after the death of most First Battalion officers.

Lieutenant Turner Turnbull (D/505) and his few brave troopers, who fought almost as a lost patrol for most of the day, had stopped the Germans from getting into Ste. Mere Eglise from the main Cherbourg-Paris Route 13 highway on the Neuville au Plain north side. They were attacked by tanks, a self-propelled gun (SP) from 500 yards range (that got a direct hit on our bazooka man), heavy and light machine-guns, mortars and 88's. Even though outnumbered four to one, not including German tanks and cannons, Turnbull and the Second Battalion were not about to back down. And they didn't.

The 505 Third Battalion that earlier rolled into the center of the town at 0400 hours, killing eleven enemy and taking 30 prisoners, later suffered the brunt of the efforts from those Germans who had managed to flee out of town. The Third Battalion was required to defend an attack coming from the south later that day by as the Germans attempted to re-capture Ste. Mere Eglise.

Finally, at 2100 hours as darkness was approaching, General Ridgway got a radio message, in the clear, to the 4th Division to get their tanks and infantry off the beaches and give the 82nd some large 75mm and 155mm artillery support as well as ammunition. At the end of D-Day, while still broad daylight between 2110h and 2120h, 75 "Mission Elmira" gliders landed in Ste. Mere

Eglise area. Both the Waco CG4A and British Horsa type also arrived after dark at 2300h and 2310h with another 100 gliders flying in, some 175 gliders arriving in two hours. Along came additional artillery-men of the 80th Airborne Anti-Aircraft Battery, 82nd Division Artillery, 307 Medical company, A/307 Engineers, 319th and 320th Glider Field Artillery, 82nd HQ with vehicles, the 82nd Signal Company with much needed communication gear, and the 82nd Reconnaissance platoon and other units. These gliders had no better luck then those that came in before daylight on D-Day at 0400 hours. The short fields led to many crashes into or through the hedgerows. But a good deal of their precious cargo was recovered and moved out to strategic points under the cover of night. Of the 175 gliders landing between those hours, 137 gliders were damaged or destroyed with death or serious injury to the soldiers on board.

At 0130 hours on 7 June the 80th AAA Battalion official log shows that they had two 57mm guns from "C" Battery in position at the la Fiére Bridge and one 57mm at the Chef-du-Pont Bridge (presumably from the Horsa glider No. IG887 that landed in the midst of Captain Creek's battle for the Chef-du-Pont Bridge). The 80th AAA Commander, Lieutenant Colonel Raymond E. Singleton landed at 0700 hours on 7 June and reported in with the 508 PIR Battalion dug in at the railroad crossing.

Except for the platoon outpost guards and the medical doctors most 82nd warriors were tucked in about as deep down as they could shovel, getting what rest they could after practically no sleep for over forty-four hours. They would need the rest. The next morning the boys at la Fiére would take part in one of the worst battles that "A" Company and the First Battalion would ever experience.

Chapter 5

D-DAY PLUS ONE

After a night with a bright moon, the dawn of D-Day Plus One brought forth an early morning mortar attack on the "A" Company 505 positions on both sides of the Manoir near the foot of the Merderet River. Further back Colonel Lindquist's 508 PIR men were dug-in along the railroad embankment. The Germans owned the western real estate across the causeway in Cauquigny. They had been seriously mauled the afternoon before and it was just as obvious to any combat-wise buck private or as it was to General Gavin that the German 91st Air Landing Division was going to mass its forces to get into and through Ste. Mere Eglise and try to push the Americans off Utah Beach.

They didn't waste any time on that fateful Wednesday morning of June 7, 1944.

The battleground had been cleared of the dead and wounded. "A" Company 505 PIR had lost one quarter of its men and would tie that amount again in the impending enemy attack, the worst of all to be faced. But "A" Company 505 had a lot of experience from Sicily in July 1943 when they took on six tanks at one time, knocking out two, damaging two and driving the remainder off. Captain Edwin Sayre (DSC Col. ret.) their former company commander, seriously wounded during action in Italy, had one simple but tough philosophy: "Don't back down". Lieutenant Dolan, was cut from the same cloth and Sayre's attitude was apparently engraved in the minds of his former "A" Company men.

During the night enemy artillery and mortars were unrelenting. In the la Fiére area artillery took out 6 more A/505 men along with some of the supporting 507 and 508 troopers. Private Kelly Byars took care of wounded me at the aid station during the night. Byars never slept and evidenced no fear of shelling while he went about his work. With daylight at 0611 hours 185 C-47 aircraft dropped re-supply parachute bundles on DZ "O". At least half of the bundles were recovered, but many landed to the southwest and into German hands. No ammunition had yet been brought into the First Battalion area by the 4th Division, which landed at Utah Beach on D-Day. No tanks had arrived on, or anywhere near, the la Fiére Manoir area. The only re-supply came from our patrolling men, scavengers who took ammunition from wounded men at the rear medical aid stations and retrieved more from the innards of crashed gliders. The men of the 82nd Airborne would face the enemy on D+1 on their own. At 0611 to 0629 an air re-supply drop was finally made.

Lieutenant Colonel Mark Alexander, who took over the First Battalion 505 after the Germans were defeated at the la Fiére Bridge, got a thorough "welcome aboard" the day before and early the next morning when enemy artillery started pounding the area. The orders for First Battalion 505 were to stay where they were and stop the next attack across the causeway. Every man in the unit knew Jerry was coming. The 507 Company that Gavin placed on the right (north) river embankment the night before went to the flank of A/505 under control of Captain R. D. Rae. The other half of Maloney's 507 reinforcements, that came up from Chef-du-Pont after the A/505 la Fiére tank battle, were positioned on the south side of the Manoir. However, because of the signs of a likely attack just north of Ste. Mere Eglise those 200 men were pulled out of both the right and left flanks of A/505 and joined Lindquist's 508 and 507 force marching east on orders from Gavin. No one told 'Red Dog' Dolan that these 507 men were on his flank, so they were not missed when pulled out on 7 June. Like the day before, the men of "A" Company had no idea that there were 507 or 508 troopers in the vicinity.

"A" Company which bore the brunt of the D-Day cross-causeway attack had its first platoon dug in deep, but in a wide open and exposed area above the river bank and in the hedgerow ditch right on the north side of the bridge. Corporal Dave Billington

49

told First Sergeant Matteson about the exposure of his men. Matteson and Dolan moved some men back to a safer position, gaining a better field of fire in the process. At just about daylight, we were visited by a squad from Company "B" 307th Parachute Engineers, with two machine-gun crews from the 505 First Battalion Headquarters Company. Second Lieutenant William A. Oakley had personally laid out the positions of these machine-gun crews and the 307 Engineers, now acting as rifle men, inside the "A" Company perimeter so as to get maximum cross fire on the causeway during the attack we knew was to come shortly. Enemy artillery continued unabated as these re-deployments went on. Platoon Staff Sergeant Lawrence F. Monahan was fatally wounded by mortar fire while we prepared for the enemy attack.

The day before we observed the German infantry coming toward us huddled behind the approaching tanks on the causeway. When those tanks were destroyed we had a field day shooting at the exposed infantry. In fact, most of us were practically out of M1 rifle ammo until Private Richard Reye and a few hustlers distributed collected bandoleers of M1 rounds, bazooka ammunition and boxes of machine-gun ammo. Dolan was with the first platoon. The second platoon, with First Lieutenant Wayne Presnell, was on the left of the bridge partly behind the forward stone wall and also down on the south side of the river embankment so as to shoot cross fire onto the tree lined causeway.. About 20 mis-dropped 507 and 508 men began wading across the flooded marsh from the west side across from the Manoir, just as daylight broke. About half were easily cut down by the German machine-gun and rifle fire from the causeway embankment from the western shore.

The German tanks that were on the other (west) side of the causeway had been rumbling back and forth most of the night and we could clearly hear the German soldiers talking. Obviously, they were digging in on the causeway but after the flogging they took the day before they were not about to come against us in the middle of the night, especially as it was a bright moonlit night except for the occasional cloud cover.

At 1000 hours on D Plus One the enemy attack across the causeway began. It was once again heralded by the slow approach of two of the same type of Renault tanks with another two hundred foot-soldiers following behind and inter-spaced with the tanks. Two additional German tanks followed for a total of four supporting the onslaught. The war was on again.

The "A" Company men in the front line, on both the east side and next to the bridge, as well as with the Headquarters, "B" and "C" Company men that were still in the Manoir and hill positions waited alone with their thoughts. Since 0800 the mortars and heavy artillery, including the horrifying tree bursts intensified. The men were in their foxholes, but, of necessity, craned their necks looking out for the enemy approach. They were all thinking one thought. Is today the day that I get it? The men were wet and shivering from the moist ocean and marsh air. They were dirty, thirsty (with no water throats were dry), and hungry. K rations were all expended and, on top of all of those debilitating factors, more Germans were attacking than their meager stockpile of ammunition could conceivably handle.

Unless one has faced the grim reaper in the form of an oncoming enemy one can hardly understand the fear and dread that runs through the mind of a front line infantryman. You pray. You have the fear of death on your mind. You are watching armed men and tanks coming at you as well as artillery and mortar explosions and shrapnel flying through the air around you. There is no thought in your mind to get out of your hole and run because you would be cut down by rifle or shrapnel fragments. That fear doesn't end or leave you until you get a chance to open fire with your weapon directly at the enemy, in our case an enemy who wasn't more than forty yards in front of us. Then, the only thought on your mind is sighting the enemy soldier and getting off two or three round bursts until he falls. Then get another few rounds off. There are plenty of targets.

It's surprising but while sighting and shooting you are oblivious to the mortar and artillery bursts around you. One piece of shrapnel hit the very large part of my helmet and pushed my head forward into the dirt during the German attack. Fortunately, I had my helmet pushed way back to get my eye right down on the sight of my Garand rifle. The Krauts were lobbing in mortars on the first and second platoons above the river banks. The 1/505 men about 55 yards to the rear were still getting hit with artillery. It seemed to be pay back time, indeed, for the pasting we had given Jerry the day before.

The first two tanks got no farther than did the column of the prior afternoon. Peterson and the other three bazooka men met the attack head on. They were supported by a 57mm gun firing from directly above the embankment. It was an almost untenable position for an anti-tank gun, but no worse than the position taken over by A/505 Corporal Felix Ferrazzi acting as a stand-in machine-gunner of the first platoon. Ferrazzi was in fact a radio operator, but finding himself without a radio he took over from Ralph Barr, a dead machine-gunner. He took a position directly under the 57mm cannon so that both weapons would hold a line of fire directly on the bridge. The 57mm gunners told Ferrazzi to move. They told him he couldn't possibly take it there. He insisted on staying and though the blast from the 57mm rounds shook him terribly he remained at his post until his machine-gun was knocked out by mortar fire. An earlier burst had showered him with fragments and cut him badly around the head and neck. But he kept firing as long as his gun was operable.

The enemy armor was stopped almost at the very center of the bridge. By that time the lead tank was already past the firing angle of the bazooka crews' original position but Peterson and Heim, Bolderson and Pryne had dropped back inside the rifle line. Whether from a rocket or one of the 57mm shells, or both, the first tank got a disabling hit that piled up the advancing column. The German infantry which had been coming on behind the tanks was again held in check. Now, however, there was a difference in the German defensive situation. The pile-up of two dead German tanks and the burned out German truck which Presnell and the bazooka men had dragged onto the bridge the day before formed a partial barricade, giving the enemy foot soldier something to fight from behind. They made good use of the cover provided. The two forces became locked in a sudden to-the-death firefight from less than 40 yards range. A deadly range. The Germans crouched behind their tanks. The Americans made the most of their ground cover. Suddenly, the mortar fire from the west bank doubled in intensity with most of it falling among Oakley's men until they could scarcely raise their heads. Second Lieutenant Oakley was hard hit by one mortar burst and spouted so much blood from a big hole in his back that they had to get him out in the middle of the fight. Billy Owens gave him a morphine shot. Sergeant William D. Owens, a squad leader, took command of what was left of the first platoon. Oakley died behind a hedgerow; a heroic leader.

The platoon strength was dwindling so rapidly from the bullet and mortar fire that Owens found it difficult to know whether any defensive line remained. First Sergeant Robert M. Matteson, who was slightly to the rear of the rifle line was trying to steer the wounded back. He found them coming back in such numbers that he "felt like a policemen directing traffic." Sergeant Russell O'Neal saw a new replacement trooper to his third platoon get half his head taken off by an '88'. O'Neal didn't even know his name. Private John Ross also took a direct hit with an '88'. There was nothing left of him but body-parts and dog tags.

Owens stood there, conspicuously in the open and no more than 40 yards from the bridge embankment, a quietly impressive figure. He rallied his men just by the example of his own fearlessness. The close-up fire from behind the barricade of wrecked armor was taking a terrible toll on our men and the enemy mortars pounded the embankment unceasingly. More than half of the first platoon had become casualties. In Owens' own first squad only three men remained. The remainder of the "A" Company line was not in position where it could get a clear shot or give any strong support to the first platoon's position. The men continued to fire at anything that moved but they did so knowing that the issue was being decided on the ground held by Owens' platoon. If his platoon broke, the whole position would go.

The soaking wet new strays who had come into the line from across the west side of the river at dawn were the first to get out. Not all of them, but a few. Most of them had been shocked, wounded and exhausted by their experiences. Lacking that sense of personal identity or comradeship with the unit which is the final stabilizing force in moments of supreme emergency. These stragglers responded to their instinct for self-preservation. Owens was too preoccupied with other matters to make any attempt to dissuade them but he could measure the effect on his own men. These small withdrawals weakened and worried them. Maybe Dolan could pull them in. Sergeant Matteson saw a lieutenant, a stranger to "A" Company, start for the rear. "I saw a whole battalion of infantry over there this morning," said the lieutenant. "We can't stop them and it's time to get out." Matteson couldn't tell him to stay. The machine-gun ammunition supply in the front line was now down to one box per gun. The guns remained active only by the persistence of Staff Sergeant Edwin F. Wancio (the supply sergeant) who kept burrowing and crawling up to the fire line from the rear, carrying enough ammunition boxes to keep the guns fed. Elijah Starr and Harold Rose found a full box of machine-gun ammo next to their position. They never knew how it magically got there. There were no spare barrels for the guns. They were kept in such constant use that when the gunners stopped firing momentarily, the guns spat out ten or twelve additional rounds. Two of the machine-guns in the company line broke down from over-heating but Lieutenant John Otto cannibalized them on the spot and got one gun back into operation. Lieutenant Otto went to the top of the first embankment and was yelling out in over the din of falling mortar rounds enemy targets that he could plainly see, as well as firing at them.

Attrition to the men and weapons caused matters to finally reach the breaking point. Machine-gunner Oscar Queen and BAR man Dave Bullington were just about out of ammunition. Queen had fired thousands of rounds. The wounded crawled on back. More of the non-505 strays quit the ground. Half the strength of the line was gone. Owens, standing in the key position, had lost all but 15 men. At last these few began to waver as it looked hopeless with ammo running out. They said to Owens, 'let's get out, we'd better withdraw.' Owens replied, "No, we will wait for orders. We haven't been told to go." Yet he was uncertain of his own decision and felt the onrushing death of his men, so he sent his best runner over to ask Lieutenant Dolan what he had better do. Back to the remnant of the platoon came the runner with the answer. Dolan had written it out in pencil. "I don't know a better place than this to die"[9], and verbally, "Stay where you are.".

It was in these moments and in this "die hard" spirit that platoon and all of "A" Company met and passed their crisis along with the First Battalion 505 men on the perimeter. They stood their ground. Within a few minutes of Dolan's stubborn and death defying note to Owens, the Germans raised a Red Cross flag and asked for a half-hour respite to take out their wounded. Colonel Mark Alexander, 'Red Dog' Dolan and Company "A" were happy to grant this request. It gave them a chance to succor the wounds of their own men and to regroup with what little strength they had. During the heat of the battle with heavy artillery, mortar rounds and machine-gun fire coming into your position it is impossible to tell who is still alive due to the distance between foxholes. During that half hour armistice the German effort to reestablish the position along the line of the Merderet River passed into decline. The enemy infantry did not come on against the First Battalion 505 position defending the bridge. After the German first-aid parties had carried away a great many of the wounded there was no renewal of the close-up fight from behind the wrecked tanks and burnt out truck sitting in the middle of the bridge. Sporadic mortar fire and 88mm artillery continued to fall into the 1/505 and Company "A" ground throughout the remainder of the day with some further losses of 82nd Airborne men. That night, after dark, what was left of "A" Company and of the First Battalion prepared to be relieved by the 325 GIR and elements of the 507 that had just returned with Lindquist's 508 force from a long patrol to the area northeast of Ste. Mere Eglise and far from the June la Fiére bridge battle.

The Germans still occupied the causeway embankments and were securely dug in with all their machine-guns emplacements, riflemen, and mortars. Lieutenant Colonel Mark Alexander and medical aide-man Kelly Byars while looking for wounded men both dived for the same small fox hole dug in the rocky riverbank and were jammed in during a forty five minute barrage. It was an uncommon place for high ranking officers (of any rank) to do heavy physical work the same as the enlisted soldier. That is one of the reasons the enlisted men had such great respect for our airborne officers, like Kellam, McGinity, Mark Alexander, John Dolan, Generals Ridgway and Gavin. They were not averse to lugging heavy equipment around, firing any weapon or fixing a bayonet to a soldier's M1 rifle for him.

The force at the Manoir and la Fiére Bridge still had no long range firepower until late on the afternoon on 7 June. The few 81mm and 60mm mortar rounds had to be held in case of another serious enemy attack. About 1700 hours the Second Battalion of the 325 Glider Infantry Regiment (2/325) was moved into a reserve position to the rear of the 505 and attached to the 1/505. The 1/505 still occupied and controlled the la Fiére bridge under command of Mark Alexander. More mines were placed on the bridge by the wrecked tanks and truck. Along with the 2/325 came a platoon of tanks from the 4th Division's 746th Tank Bat-

55

talion (attached), also located to the rear at the bend of the roadway and out of enemy sight. An additional 75 men from the 507 came into position on the left side of the road on the knoll behind the Manoir. These were combined with Lieutenant Colonel Maloney and Captains Roy Creek and Robert Rae. They formed into three provisional company size units.

During the day on June 8th, D+2, the First Battalion 505 PIR were relieved by elements of the 507 PIR. The 1/505 then moved on over to take the positions of the Third Battalion 505 north of Granville; the 3/505 was then put in reserve.

The 325 glidermen and 507 troopers would have a day of rest from enemy attack but on 9 June the decimation of the 325 infantrymen would begin on the la Fiére causeway in a fierce battle, where the 325 positions led off to the west.

The fight which the Lindquist 508 troopers had expected near Neuville au Plain had never materialized. During the entire day Lindquist's force had seen and killed only one German and it was only toward the end of the advance that the force began to draw a scattering of mortar fire. He had reported these facts to Division Headquarters by runner. Lindquist included in his estimate that where he was and to the northeast that day, there was no enemy strength on his immediate front. The runner returned with orders to withdraw and in consequence, Lindquist led his 508 men back toward the railway line about the time that the la Fiére Bridge fight cooled off and the Germans had withdrawn. At no time while his men were along the railway bank or operating beyond it to the east had they drawn artillery fire. Lindquist and all his 508 force on the morning of 7 June, was ordered to relieve Captain Creek (507) and proceed to the Chef-du-Pont Bridge.

Company "A" prepared to move back from the Manoir and la Fiére position on the morning of 8 June. First Sergeant Matteson looked up and down the line of his Company and said to his men: "If people don't think that men get killed in war, they ought to take a look at this company." "A" Company had started with 147 able-bodied men on D-Day but their strength was now 66 less from death and serious wounds. Of the men standing in front of Matteson, 20 were wearing bandages or were awaiting medical attention. They were the lightly wounded who had seen the show through and wouldn't report to the aid stations.

One survivor more responsible than anyone else for holding the Germans back was Sergeant William D. Owens. His own account of the attack on 7 June was published by General Gavin in his book, "On to Berlin" as follows, "I had the 1st squad. We placed our antitank mines right on the top of the road where the Germans could see them, but could not miss them with their tanks. We placed our two bazooka teams where they had a good field of fire. There were two men to a team. As I recall it was about 8:00 a.m. when we first heard armored vehicles coming from across the river. We let them come on. It was an armored column with trucks of infantry. When the lead tank got approximately forty feet from the mines, the tank stopped. Then our bazooka teams let loose and both got direct hits, disabling the first tank (they were old French Renault tanks with comparatively thin armor). This blocked the road, and as there were deep ditches and water, the other tanks could only retreat. They tried to get the infantry though to knock us out. All we had was small arms and some 60mm mortars, but we succeeded in driving them back. The Germans pulled back on the other side, and in about a half hour or so, they began throwing 88's and 120mm mortars at us. They really clobbered us. All our communications were knocked out. And the fellow, Private Ross, without walkie-talkie, took a direct hit with an '88', so from then on, as far as we were concerned, we were a lost platoon. Then they sent the infantry again, and again we drove them back. Our platoon leader Lieutenant Oakley, was badly wounded (he died a few hours later). After he left, I began crawling around, getting all the ammunition and grenades from the dead and wounded, for I knew we would need every round we could get our hands on. I took stock of what weapons we had, and it turned out to be a good thing for right after that the Germans hit us again. They must have received reinforcements, for the artillery shells and mortars were coming in like machine-gun fire. I don't know how is was possible to live through it. Then the infantry came again and we gave them everything we had. The machine-gun I had was so hot it quit firing. I took Private McClatchy's BAR,(he had been wounded earlier), and I fired it until I ran out of ammunition. I then took a machine-gun that belonged to a couple of men who took a very near hit. They were killed. The gun had no tripod, so I rested it across a pile of dirt and used it. With this and one other machine-gun and a 60mm mortar, we stopped them but they had gotten to within twenty-five yards of us. I really thought we'd had it, but then they threw up a Red Cross flag and stopped firing. I quickly stood up and stopped my men. I sent a man back to see if he could find some help for us. I moved to where I could get a good view of the causeway. I estimated that I could see at least two hundred dead or wounded Germans scattered about. I don't know how many were in the river. It took them about two hours to get their wounded out, then they started shelling us again but not as bad as before. About two in the morning I heard a tank on the causeway and thought here we go again. Then I heard them trying to push the disabled tank out of the way and I knew if they succeeded we would be through, so I took a couple of Gammon grenades (plastic C) and crawled to approximately thirty or forty yards from them. It was quite dark. The first grenade I threw missed and hit the disabled tank instead of the one that was trying to move it. The Germans didn't take any more chances, they put the tank into reverse and moved back. They continued shelling us all day long, but it was sporadic."

They never tried to get the infantry across again after they raised the Red Cross flag[10].

Thanks to Company "A" and the First Battalion 505 the la Fiére Bridge position on the cast bank, which had been vigorously defended for two full days, again appeared well in hand on the morning of 8 June. Now defended by the forces of Lieutenant Colonel Maloney and backed by the newly-arrived 3rd Battalion, 325 Glider Infantry Regiment, it was well supplied with ammunition and supported by tanks and artillery. Nevertheless, no attempt was made that day to cross at la Fiére by either side. Instead, Colonel Lindquist's 508 force was shifted on 7 June to Chef-du-Pont in the mid morning on orders to organize the bridgehead there and establish contact with Colonel Shanley's men isolated on Hill 30 across the Merderet causeway. It was also to secure the left flank of the division cast of the Merderet. The latter mission was given to two companies which, without loss to themselves, cleared the Carquebut and Eturville area, taking 235 prisoners and establishing contact with the 101st Airborne Division to the south.

Colonel Lindquist did not succeed, however, in his principal mission of joining Colonel Shanley's isolated force. From Hill 30

Colonel Shanley could overlook the Merderet and the causeway running west from the Chef-du-Pont bridge but his only contact with the forces east of the river was by patrol. For purposes of supply and medical aid he was cut off by enemy dominance of the western end of the causeway. On D+1, when Colonel Shanley's force had been augmented by stray parachutists with machine-guns, a road block had been organized south of the Hill 30. The block, manned by about fifty men, covered the northern and western approaches to the causeway, both of which had been mined with German mines found in the area. But on the morning of 8 June, while the road block positions were being reorganized, the enemy attacked from the west. Unprepared at the time to defend the position and threatened with heavy losses from continuous enemy mortar fire, the Americans were withdrawn. Colonel Shanley decided that the immediate tactical value of the Hill 30 position did not warrant large sacrifices and that he was strong enough to retake the ground when necessary.

NOTES FOR CHAPTER 5:
9. The most remarkable tribute the History Officer heard paid to any soldier in the ETO was paid by Company "A" to Owens. When the company was interviewed as a body, all hands said, "The defense was saved by Owens. It was his courage and calmness which made us stick out. He carried the load." Owens is not a conspicuous-looking soldier. He is a man of medium size, rather reserved and considerably older than the average paratrooper. In the presence of the whole company, he said this, "We stuck because our leaders stuck and we knew they were sticking. Captain (promoted) Dolan was with us all the time. Such of the younger officers Alexander kept coming up into the fight. We saw General Ridgway up there and General Gavin. We knew what we were doing and that they would give us all the help they could. That did more to give us confidence than the power of our weapons." (Quoted from Historian Colonel Marshall)
10. Based on personal 1959 correspondence by General Gavin with Sgt. Owens as well as the personal account of the June 6th and 7th actions as told by the officers and men of Company "A" 505 PIR as part of the official U. S. Army history. Also verified by Robert M. Murphy the author of this 1997 documentary and a participant of the la Fiére battles. Lieutenant Dolan recommended a DSC for Owens but he never got it.

Chapter 6
ADVANCE ACROSS THE MARSH

While the Timmes 2/507 force was stuck in the orchard on D+2 a two man patrol consisting of Lieutenant John W. Marr and Private First Class Norman V. Carter left the orchard in the afternoon and crossed from the west over to the northeast side of the marsh with the help of directions provided by a Frenchman. Marr got a jeep and while driving he ran into General Ridgway on the road and explained the Timmes 507 position and the fact they could not go in any direction and needed reinforcements. General Ridgway ordered the First Battalion 325, commanded by Major Teddy H. Sanford, to go across the marsh on the northeast sunken road and attack in concert with Timmes to take the western end of the la Fiére causeway.

The 507 Regimental commander Colonel Millett was also ordered to join with Timmes in a joint 325 and 507 force to drive the Germans out of the Cauquigny bridgehead and clear the western end of the causeway.

The Millett Force had no success in their attempt to join with Major Sanford. They were separated and with Colonel Millet was captured. The 1/325 crossed over the marsh and as it advanced it drew fire from the 'Gray Castle', a substantial stone structure overlooking the battlefield from a rise to the north. They did manage to subdue the enemy. The rest of the 1/325 went on to join the Timmes force heading toward Cauquigny and soon ran into strong enemy defenses and were thrown back before dawn with heavy losses to Timmes' men. This was after a night of close-in fighting and the separation of the 1/325 force. By daylight the men remaining had to stay with Timmes, although some re-crossed the river.

The Germans who were at first driven out of the "Gray Castle" now counter-attacked with the help of substantial reinforcements. It was now broad daylight. The 1/325 had been badly shot up and had orders to return back across the sunken road or stay in the Timmes defense zone. This was the first time the 1/325 had been in combat. The night attempt to infiltrate across the marsh and turn to the south was ambitious for the untried unit. It did not succeed. One of the 82nd Airborne Division's most gallant heroes came to the fore during this firefight. PFC Charles DeGlopper (C/325) bravely defended his platoon while they were taking cover from a large enemy attacking force. De Glopper told his platoon comrades to get on the other side of a hedgerow while he stood (all of six feet six inches tall) in the middle of the road firing his BAR directly at the attacking German infantry. He was hit by enemy bullets yet continued to fire and reloaded another clip. He fell to his knees and was still firing as every German cut loose on him, killing him but allowing his comrades to withdraw. As a result of Charles De Glopper's heroic stand, at the loss of his life and above and beyond the call of duty, he was awarded the Congressional Medal of Honor.

When Brigadier General Gavin heard of the failure of the 1/325's attempt to capture the bridgehead he made a final decision to cross the Merderet at the la Fiére bridge causeway. The Third Battalion 325 Glider Infantry Regiment (3/325) would spearhead the attack to be supported by Captain Robert Rae's reinforced 507 Parachute Infantry Provisional Company along with Captains Roy Creek and Captain Brockonecke's Provisional Companies with Lieutenant Colonel Arthur Maloney's leadership in the event the leading 3/325 Companies faltered or were mowed down. They hoped they would have some American tanks to help them. However, the tanks of the 746th did not arrive until the 325 men were already across the causeway.

Attack Across la Fiére Causeway 9 June

On the morning of 9 June the 3/325 came out of reserve at the east railroad crossing and moved into and around the Manoir position. The 507 was placed on the Merderet River bank south of the bridge at the Manoir. Captain Rae was told to be ready and wait for a signal from Maloney to get up out of his position and take off across the causeway with his paratroopers. Maloney was to stick close to Gavin within 600 yards of the bridge.

General Gavin was in command of the attack. Both he and General Ridgway met with the 90th Division Artillery commander, Brigadier General John M. Divine, and got assurance that the 90th's large-caliber 155mm cannons would rake the west side of the Cauquigny causeway and mortars would traverse the causeway east to west. At 1030h the artillery bombardment would begin and at 1045h a smoke barrage would be laid down. Gavin asked the tank commander to move his tanks up closer to the bend in the road where they could not be seen by the enemy but could fire their supporting cannons.

The Third Battalion 325 men were now in position all through the Manoir and behind the large stone wall close to the bridge. There was a gap in the wall that the enemy had spotted and were firing through. Company G 325 was going to lead the attack with Companies E and F/325 to follow. The Battalion Commander told Gavin he was sick and couldn't go forward, so Gavin relieved him on the spot. The 1030h outgoing artillery began and fire was immediately returned by the enemy. The 90th Division 345th Field Artillery Battalion 155mm cannons fired continuously for 15 minutes. Company "A", 746th Tank Battalion Shermans moved behind the Manoir and fired. The Germans began a withering fusillade of machine-gun fire from across the west side raking our positions all over the Manoir and buildings. The Manoir house was again blasted by heavy artillery, blowing away the front door. The sounds of the guns and artillery was deafening as the 3/325 moved toward the bridge to cross at 1045h under the cover of the promised smoke barrage. The Germans knew the Americans were going to attack and had a reinforced regiment on the other side with many mortars and artillery pieces in support.

At 1045h after a few smoke shells (about as much smoke from a pack of Lucky Strikes), the attack began. Captain Sauls had previously moved his men out of their protective ditches and around the back of the Manoir and the big shoulder-high protection of the stone wall. They only had to run past a seven foot gap in the wall while an enemy machine-gun played its fire through the gap. The men were now piled up and in tight so that two platoons were compressed into a five yard line. Enemy small arms fire was ricocheting off the wall, from buildings and along the river bank where the 507 men were deployed. Just before jump-off time, Major Arthur W. Gardner the new Battalion Commander came out into the position to talk to Sauls at the head of the column along with staff Sergeant Wilfred L. Ericsson and Lieutenant Donald B. Wason. They were to lead the 82nd Airborne Division attack across the la Fiére Causeway. Sauls raised his hand and gave the signal, yelling out, "Go". Captain Sauls ran forward and became the first man leading off on the east side with Wason and Ericsson behind him. Heavy enemy fire hit them from both flanks and from the front. These G/325 glider infantrymen had 750 yards to go across the causeway shelled by mortar rounds. Sauls told his men to run straight up as fast as possible as it was the best chance they had to make it across. A BAR man from the 2nd Squad went across right behind Ericsson. They all reached the western end, totally winded but unharmed. Shells were falling only 25 to 30 yards beyond them.

Sergeant Ericsson went to the left roadway with his BAR and the rest of the squad that got over with them. Captain Sauls stopped at the end of the causeway to direct the 30 men following him into new positions. For some reason, as far as he could see to the bend in the road halfway back on the causeway, the men of his company were not following. The trouble and stoppage occurred right after Sauls et. al. took off. Private Melvin L. Johnson was shot through the head by the enemy machine-gun firing through the gap in the Manoir stone wall. His body, falling across the passageway, shocked and stopped the remaining men of G Company and the entire battalion behind them. They stayed unmoving at this spot for nearly 10 minutes until Lieutenant Frank E Amino got up and yelled out at his crouching men, "Let's go on and kill the sons of bitches" as he ran across the gap in the wall and out onto the causeway. Some of the men got up and followed but some stayed glued behind the wall.

The ones who started out were bogged down by some of the dead and wounded now laying on the causeway road. Some men stopped and laid by the roadside. They were killed by the artillery and mortars raining down instead of running for the other side. Those following began to slow up on seeing the bodies they almost stopped the advance. They couldn't linger, though as the longer the fight on the causeway lasted, the more 3/325 men would be killed or wounded.

The 3rd platoon of B Company, 307 Engineer Battalion and 2nd Platoon of A/307 were on the Causeway during the attack across the la Fiére Bridge on 9 June. The 1st Platoon of A/307 at 1045h on 9 June worked on three knocked-out German tanks, mines and other debris from the bridge and causeway under heavy indirect fire. The brave "A" and "B" 307 paratroopers were supposed to wait until the 325 GIR and the 507 had attacked west across the causeway to take the bridgehead at Cauquigny. They did their engineering job during the 82nd and 90th Division artillery barrage on the causeway and Cauquigny hamlet. Unfortunately they missed one mine on the embankment.

An American Sherman tank had started its advance over the bridge but struck the mine by the roadside veering around the wrecked German tank. The explosion disabled the tank and wounded seven men from the weapons platoon. Staff Sergeant George F. Myers, who was a section leader of the mortars, was struck above the eye and almost blinded. Myers nevertheless jumped up off the ground, leading his men across the causeway. Myer's soldiers begged him to go back as he was bleeding profusely. He refused their entreaties.

There were soon twenty to thirty casualties strung out along the road while more men slowly crossed over, picking their way over the fallen. The enemy mortar fire continued to rain in along with small arms fire threading the causeway and Manoir area. The situation on the causeway soon became a problem for unit leadership from division commander down to sergeant. Officers and non-coms were trying to get the wounded back off the causeway while at the same time get the faint hearted moving over the dead soldiers to clear the road of enemy.

The brave souls who were the first to cross all the way over were practically alone on the other side and at the mercy of the heavily armed enemy. Captain Sauls looked about him. He was aware that scarcely thirty men had come over with him to close with the enemy. And most of these men had already disappeared into the fields and among the hedgerows to gain cover as they proceeded toward their assigned objective.

Lieutenant Wason[11] had gone straight up the main road with eight men following him at a safe distance. During his dash across the causeway Wason had seen an enemy machine-gun firing straight down the road towards the bridge. He wanted that gun. The time soon came when getting it meant a straight dash across open ground toward the enemy emplacement. Wason told the other men he would go it alone. His initiative would succeed at the cost of his life. Wason's grenade knocked the gun out just as one of the German gunners shot him dead. Sauls' runner, Private First Class Frank Thurston, had gone on with Wason's party and, witnessing his death, noted another machine-gun firing from farther up the road. He returned to Sauls and said, "Sir, I know where there is a machine-gun nest. Can I go get it?" Sauls told him to go ahead. He went on up to a position near the first road intersection, lay down behind a hedge and shot the enemy crew dead one at a time with his Garand rifle. He returned to Sauls laughing out loud. "I got the bastards," he announced.

In turning down the first trail leading left along the river bank, Sergeant Ericsson had motioned to his BAR man, Private First Class James D. Kittle, to take position at the high corner of the first field on the right and get ready to fire. Ericsson and some others ran down the trail. Ericsson planned that he and his men would grenade the enemy from out of the fire positions behind the hedgerow running parallel to the trail. Then, as the Germans fell back through the field, Kittle could mow them down with his BAR. It almost worked that way. Right at the beginning two Germans popped out from behind the hedgerow with their helmets rattling and their hands up. Ericsson thumbed them back toward the causeway and they went obediently, without guard. The Americans went on a few more yards and then threw grenades over the hedges. The enemy responded in kind. Ericsson and his men dove flat. It seemed to them as the German grenades exploded that the concussion was extremely slight and could not do them much harm. Another dozen Germans came from behind the hedge, hands raised. They too were motioned back toward the causeway—and off they went. These developments built confidence in Ericsson's men. There was more grenading and more surrenders. In short order, the prisoner exodus from the field became general and all resistance ceased in that small area. Others of Sauls men had proceeded in the same way against the hedgerow positions along the main road. Some additional strength, which resulted in a large number of surrenders, had come with the belated arrival of Lieutenant Amino and his platoon who had been delayed by the dead soldier incident at the wall. Sauls sent about two and a half squads along in the direction Wason had gone, thus establishing the right flank of Company "G". They set up a fire position along the main road to cover the fields toward the southwest. They also placed some of their automatic weapons to counter the fire coming from the buildings to right of the road, around the Cauquigny church.

One of Amino's men, Tech Sergeant John P. Kneale worked his way up to the first fork in the main road. He stood there waving his arms back and forth at the other men: "Come on! We've got the goddamn bastards on the run." Sniper fire kicked up the all around him. He paid no heed and kept on yelling. The men moved around and past him. To Sauls, Kneale's stand was the "prettiest sight of the day" and one of the most effective individual actions he'd seen during the struggle. He knew that in his exposed position, Kneale was already pushing his luck and asking for a bullet. His own nerves became taut from this exhibition and he finally ran forward the necessary distance and gave Kneale a personal order to take cover.

Ericsson and his men made a temporary withdrawal after proceeding about 100 yards down the trail. They had just about exhausted their ammunition supply and Ericsson figured he needed a few more men. He nearly reached the main road when a bullet hit him in the back and put him out of the fight.

When another platoon of Company G reached the west bank. The company built a right flank anchor along the road while some of the men worked south along the edge of the swamp, clearing the enemy from the field.

The men of E/325 were ordered to follow Company "G" across under orders to deploy to the right of the main road and clear out the ground north along the river and around the Cauquigny church. Despite the fact that its numbers were seriously depleted in the crossing, Company "E" carried out its mission with relative ease. The Germans, caught around Cauquigny by the supporting fire of the 507 Parachute Infantry from the far east shorelines, were eager to surrender. Company "E" then swept the few buildings on the north of the road and reached its objective line.

Company "F" had the mission of following companies "G" and

"E" to mop up. However, when it crossed the causeway, the bridgehead had not been deepened to the extent where mop-up operations were required. On the initiative of its commander, the company therefore struck out west along the main road to push out the center of the bridgehead.

By now General Gavin had become concerned over the congestion on the causeway and the very slow movement of troops across it. Over an hour had elapsed. In the absence of any radio or runner reports from the west bank, Gavin concluded that the 325th Glider Infantry was faltering in its attack. General Gavin was watching and listening to the actions across the causeway during the G/325 and E/325 crossing, noting all of the dead and wounded that he could see before the bend in the causeway. Many 325 men sought shelter on the embankment, a choice which actually subjected them to enemy rifle fire from both sides of the western shore as well as the devastating mortars and 88mm barrage falling on the Manoir and causeway. After an hour, Gavin saw that the 325 attack was not going smoothly, and, in his judgment it was losing the initiative to carry the day. He could not afford to be pushed back. The ground to the west of the Manoir had to be taken that day. Because Gavin hadn't the slightest idea of what was going on across the causeway at Cauquigny (which was in good, but too few hands) he called to Captain Robert Rae and told him, "all right, go ahead! you've got to go," Rae took this to mean that the 325 charge had failed. Gavin had said to Maloney and Rae that morning that if the 325 failed the 507 men were to charge across the causeway and take anyone left on it across with them. Captain Rae had no idea that there were "G" and "E" Company men already across and beyond the Cauquigny church. On receiving a direct order from General Gavin, Rae took between 80 and 100 men of the 507 PIR into a hail of bullets and artillery. They immediately ran into stragglers knotted up under the protection of the destroyed tanks. The explosions were deafening but Rae and his men hailed to the others to follow them across.

Another 325 officer, Captain Harney was in the process of getting his men out from behind the wrecked tanks when Rae and his men were approached. The narrow causeway road was so jammed with men and bodies it was almost impossible to pass with the heavy weapons of Headquarters Company. You had to pick your way along the causeway, zigzagging around and over bodies. A young 325 Lieutenant, James D. Owens, who had his helmet blown off his head was telling knotted up groups of 325 men that, "We're all going to the other side. I think you had better come along. It will be better for all of us over there." Owen's straightforward advice worked well and encouraged some men to rise up and follow him.

Captain Rae and his men moved along the road as rapidly as they could. They knew speed was their best protection. Some of Rae's men were wounded. Lieutenant Wisner, the 507 Regimental S2 officer who went along with Rae, said that the scene gradually began to resemble ".. an escalator, two streams of men on the inside trying to run forward and on the outer side streams of wounded trickling back." It was difficult to distinguish between the corpses and litter cases as one walked by. The medical aid men were among the fallen, bandaging the wounded as fast as they could.

The German prisoners that were taken by the first arriving men of G and E/325 were now being directed across the causeway with their hands held high in the air. Unfortunately, some were killed by confused soldiers. The prisoners walked past the advancing 507 paratroopers. It did not occur to the 507 paratroopers that other Americans were up ahead and had captured these men. However, on reaching the west end of the causeway the 507 men drew rifle fire from the edge of the swamp, apparently from enemy missed by the G/325 group. The Germans were beaten off. Captain Harney's remaining Headquarters Company got across within 15 minutes and he took his force straight down the road to establish his group along the high ground at the Cauquigny side of the bridgehead. Rae and his men decided to push right along in the same direction. More 325 and 507 men arrived as they were being directed across by Colonel Lewis (325) and both Ridgway and Gavin. In fact, when Lieutenant Lee C. Travelstead's heavy weapons Company (325) started to cross, he saw General Ridgway trying, on the fire swept causeway, to clear the wrecked U. S. tank off the roadway. With their heavy weapons Travelstead's men crossed over without stopping to fire.

At this point in time, Colonel Lewis had put up such a squawk about the lack of tank support that the 746th Shermans were finally brought into play. At about noon the Shermans came down the hill and started across the causeway. The wounded were moved to the side of the embankment stragglers while followed behind the tanks. Some of the 325 Command Post officers were setting up the CP in a field on the west side when a friendly tank fired into the field. It failed to hit anyone. Four jeeps and trailers loaded with ammunition soon crossed over to the west side and dumped their loads. The jeep supply column, with Sergeant Clarence A. Knutson in charge, made the re-supply run most of the afternoon along with taking the very seriously wounded back in the jeeps and trailers.

Although the 507 and 325 men were over the west side they had no cohesive force or overall commander. The men went about their work as separate units. Captains Rae and Harney sorted out the battle plan. Rae and his men would move down the road to the left and secure the high ground in a defensive position. Lieutenant White and his eighteen men were to go to the right and try to locate some of the 1/325 that got pinned down at dawn near Timmes' position and then take up a defensive position. Travelstead arrived with his heavy machine-guns and mortars. Rae split his force. Some went to the left while he and his group went straight down the road to le Motey. Captain Sauls G/325, the first to cross over, had also gone to the left side road and were doing well except his men were low on ammunition. He had no communications except passing the word along from man to man. Sauls got word from a runner to report back to the end of the causeway where he met Colonel Lewis and General Ridgway. While Sauls was giving his report, along came PFC Kenneth Lynn with 25 prisoners he'd captured within 100 feet of the spot where the officers were talking.

Meanwhile, in Sauls absence Sergeant Kneale and PFC Will E. Dickens were under heavy machine-gun fire. They set up their machine-gun and stopped the enemy fire. Dickens continued to fire and didn't see a grenade lobbed at him. Shrapnel struck him in many places and although bleeding profusely Dickens continued to fire until he died. Sauls ordered the 81mm to open fire across the hedgerow but Major Gardner, now the new CO of 3/325, countermanded that order because the 325/507 troops were too close and the mortar fire might kill our own men. Sauls got hit and was bleeding badly but he stayed on duty until he lost too much blood. A Sherman tank arrived on the scene and began shooting up the hedgerows.

A medium tank joined the group and moved along the parallel road shooting up the hedgerows as it rolled forward. Captain Sauls' men were just about out of ammunition so he sent a few stalwart soldiers back to get the some from the wounded or any stragglers they came across. In the meantime, the enemy remained steadfast. It was bullet for bullet and life for life and the enemy had to be shot in their foxholes one-by-one during the advance. Staff Sergeant Roger F. Bertoloni took five Germans and one officer as prisoners. Bertoloni fired so constantly, his machine-gun barrel burnt out and he went back and got another gun to deal with an enemy machine-gun. Every time he or his men moved that enemy gun would fire. When he stopped, it would stop, so as to not give away its position. Just as Bertoloni left a 60mm mortar wiped out the enemy machine-gun spraying his location. Sergeant James Malak and Leo Kahlreiser had fired their 60mm mortar 25 yards behind the pinned down 325 men and dropped their rounds in a 100 yard range between the 60mm and Bertoloni's machine-gun. The Germans were either killed or didn't like the 'attitude' of the glidermen; in any case that machine-gun disappeared. Sauls' wound was now so bad he turned the Company over to Lieutenant Thomas E. Goodson (later killed) who carried on.

The tank assisting in the attack had its machine-gun jam. It withdrew and dropped back out of the fight. A second tank was advancing in the gap when German mortars dropped a shell right in front of it. That tank commander figured they would eventually drop one right down his hatch so he turned the tank around, heading for another spot that was not so exposed. Sergeant Knutson, a modern day Gunga Din, appeared again with his jeep and a trailer load of ammunition. Knutson got the details on a German anti-tank gun location and reported it back to the artillery. The G/325 men went ahead for 300 yards and found no Germans so they turned to the main road where they were again stopped by machine-gun fire. Goodson sent PFC Leonard Reel on a wide sweep of the hedgerows and he came out at the rear of the German's firing position. In ten minutes Reel returned with 30 prisoners marching in columns of threes with their "*Hande Hoch*" in the air. It was now 1500 hours.

Backing up in time now, while the 325 was having its many

independent battles with the enemy after crossing the causeway, Captain Robert Rae and his men, along with Captain James M. Harvey F/325, were heading for the small hamlet of le Motey. Before getting to le Motey the front of his column was hit with 88mm artillery. Only a few men were wounded as they were around and derived some protection from some buildings. Rae immediately got out of the artillery target area and went looking for a tank to get a radio to our artillery. While looking for the tank, Rae also ran into General Ridgway and Colonel Lewis at the Cauquigny church and gave them a report. Rae returned to le Motey with the intent of trying to get to Amfreville but had no luck. The 507 troopers finally drove out the Germans and occupied le Motey, at which was a key crossroads. General Gavin, who was in the area reported, .. "The German fire was fierce. I was walking bent over in a grain field when I suddenly noticed the stalks being cut as though by a giant invisible scythe. I had not realized that the fire was quite that intense, and got down on all fours. I reached Captain Rae and told him what I wanted him to do, and he went ahead with the attack and occupied le Motey. On the way back I encountered an 81mm. mortar squad in the process of withdrawing. I turned them around and ordered them to report to Captain Rae, telling them where he was. It took about two hours to get the situation back under control. But we did succeed."

Unfortunately, Rae was later ordered to pull back into the Cauquigny church area to set up a line of his paratroopers as a defense against a possible German counterattack in force. The enemy seemed to have an inexhaustible supply of mortar and artillery rounds. With the 507 withdrawal out of le Motey it left a wide gap between "F" and "G" Companies of the 325 GIR. These two Companies were constantly discovering German patrols slipping between gaps in their lines. In fact, F/325 found itself so exposed they decided they'd better move back a couple of hedgerows and form a stable firing line. The men of Company "E" thought the F/325 was in retreat and some men scrambled out as fast as they could go. However, the panic was checked when a paratrooper lieutenant, not with the Rae group, pulled his Colt .45 and told them to, "keep your goddammed asses right where they are". The panic was over. They got the word it was not a withdrawal and went right back to E/325. Again, proof was on hand that lack of communication and one or two uninformed men can lead a pack to pull out.

Sergeant John Harrison was allowed to pass after he explained to the unknown pistol waving lieutenant that he badly needed to set up his 81mm mortars at a better spot. During the movements of the 325 men, front to back and side to side, the German artillery did not cease. Throughout the fight, it became obvious that being fired at through a hedgerow can be deadly, as an ordinary riflemen, laying still, can pick off two or three men before they see him. Then he's gone before one can get a grenade lobbed over the hedge or mount any reaction.

Captain Rae's men had also made contact with Lieutenant Colonel Timmes' immobile 507 force stuck on the west-side orchard north of the Cauquigny church. As a result of the attack across the la Fiére Causeway the German commander, who had Timmes pinned down in the same spot for four days, must have decided he needed additional forces to defend the 3/325 over the causeway attack. He pulled out the Germans holding Timmes inside the orchard. Rae just walked in to Timmes position without any enemy in sight. Some of the First Battalion 325 that went across the marsh and had their first combat mission just before dawn got caught after daylight and were also dug in with Timmes 2/507 men. As they were in the right place to take up a defensive position on the right side of the causeway (north), they were ordered to stay put in the same spot they had been occupying.

Before the battle ended the senior 82nd Commanders at Cauquigny saw a tank dashing to the rear. They became quite apprehensive and got prepared for a mass exodus touched off by the retreating tank. Instead, some ten minutes later, the same tank returned at speed. It had been gathering all kinds of ammunition and guns from the far side. Fortunately new supplies of ammunition were on hand to replenish the supplies to the men of the 325 who were just about fresh out.

NOTES FOR CHAPTER 6:
11. From S.L.A. Marshall, July 1944 interview of 325.

Chapter 7
LAST ENEMY ATTACK AND *FINIS*

After the lines were adjusted and settled by 1500 hours the defense lines of the 325 and 507 were finally somewhat orderly. About 1800 hours, an enemy artillery barrage along the entire front occupied by the 325 and 507 began with heavy force of impact and explosions.

A large amount of enemy mortar fire began raining in on Companies "E" and "F" 325 with most of it hitting Captain Harney's men. Harney, in the front of the line, could see the German infantry crossing the open fields, forming up for a new attack. Major Gardner of 3/325 had promised more support in the form of reinforcements but none appeared. The men ducked in their holes while the mortars were falling on them but when it ceased they quickly rose up and fired at the enemy, full blast. They beat off that attack even before the American artillery could help out. Fortunately, a tank gave them support with its machine-gun and cannon.

They were a lonely group until the 1/325, now free to move about, came up to the line with G/325 ready to plug the gap. Captain Rae and his men had been put in reserve but they were also under mortar fire. Most of the Germans who got up close in this last attack were killed on the spot. By 1900 hours the 325 GIR men that were supposed to go over the causeway were over there. The men of the 3/325 and 1/325 had been through as terrible a battle as possible and had whipped the enemy. May found their last resting place in the Normandy military cemeteries.

The Battle Winds Down

At 2100 hours General Gavin found Captain Rae digging himself a foxhole for the night. Rae had most certainly earned his pay during the action of that morning and afternoon. The incoming mortar fire was still falling. Gavin told Rae, "I want you to take your men and go forward." Rae asked, "How far?" "Go to town." So Robert Rae left his position got his 507 troops and proceeded to le Motey. He had no opposition except sniper fire. They got to le Motey just before dark without any skirmishing and were not engaged that night. Most of Rae's 507 Provisional Company paratroopers had come through the day with little harm but they did every job assigned to them. On the right Captain Harney was making his final advance on le Motey with three tanks and support to the right of the main road. This was the same area where E/325 got shot up about noon time. Second Lieutenant Leo J. Fitzmartin had two tanks blast away at hedgerows and a few houses but the German machine-guns were still in operation. It was still clear and daylight. Fitzmartin decided that they could easily flank that gun , so he had four enlisted men follow behind him. In the center of the field (the worst place to be in a hedgerow battle) the German machine-gun killed the four men and hit Fitzmartin who then played dead. The gun did not fire again and no one tried to take it out that night. Fitzmartin could hear the Germans talk all night but he couldn't move or get back to his lines and his men obviously thought him to be dead. At 0700 the next morning on 10 June his platoon moved across the field and found him alive. The enemy machine-gun was gone without a trace.

The occupation of le Motey was otherwise without incident. Harney and Rae built a solid defense zone with heavy machine-guns. However, after the battle and just as it was getting dark, the tanks took off due to sporadic 88mm fire along the road. Although the le Motey location was beyond the Cauquigny bridgehead it was not attacked. Both sides of the bridgehead were shelled all night.

Relief Force

At 0200 hours on 10 June Colonel Sitler was notified to provide guides to escort the newly-arrived 357th Infantry Regiment of the 90th Division who were going to pass through the 325 GIR positions and cross the Merderet. At 0400 hours the 2/357 started across the la Fiére Causeway and moved into as many foxholes of the 325 as possible. Just as A/505 and the First Battalion 505 had denied any German to cross the la Fiére bridge since 1030 hours on 6 June, the 3/325 and provisional 507 Company had, again, never allowed the enemy access over the "bridgehead".

Lieutenant General Heinz Hellmich, commanding the German 243rd Division and elements of the 709th and 91st Division, was ordered to hold the Montebourg-Quieneville line at all costs. The German 84th Corps requested aircraft against the big U. S. Navy guns which were assisting the 4th Division, progressing up the east coast. Hellmich got little air support although German aircraft were present on rare occasion. The American supplies coming in off the Utah, Omaha and the British beaches were building up every hour.

The 82nd Airborne Division paratroopers and glidermen continued the fight everyday until July 11th when they went into First Army reserve and were moved to Utah Beach for transport back to England. The 505 got many of its wounded and hospitalized men returned to the regiment. For some, it was just in time to get in on the 17 September 1944 combat jump over Grosbeek, Holland as part of Operation 'Market-Garden'.

The Merderet River barrier, the Louis Leroux Manoir de la Fiére and the little bridge over the causeway have stirring memories for us. We were the lucky ones. For many of our comrades it was their last memory.

Chapter 8

RETURN TO NORMANDY

I take the reader forward to January 1961. I was working as a Boston trial lawyer and the local county campaign manager for newly elected President John F. Kennedy. Along with three other 505 PIR combat veterans I went back to Normandy (and Holland). At Paris we rented a car and drove to Ste Mere Eglise. We didn't know a singal person there; all we knew was that the Mayor's wife had been tending the graves of Americans killed in and around the town, buried in the small military cemetery nearby.

We parked our auto and visited the famous Ste Mere Eglise (St. Mary's) church built at the time William the Conqueror, of Normandy, left to return to England in 1066. On the steeple tower of this very same church our good friend John Steele of the 505 PIR caught his parachute at about 1:15 AM on 6 June 1944. It is a beautiful church full of history, and a nice quiet place to reflect on our comrades who were killed in action here, some sixteen years prior to our visit. Right then and there in that church I forgot my fifteen-hour work days, my wife and four kids, along with the bills, and politics, as my mind brought forth the many different faces of many of my lost comrades as I prayed in this ancient, dark, and cold church.

That kind of nostalia had not been part of my experience before this moment, even through I had been to many 82nd Memorial dinners to honor our dead. The eerie feeling at that moment of prayer gave me a sense that I was closer at that moment to my buddies and could, in the eye of my mind, tell them what I'd been doing since VE Day and that I had not forgotten them, and never would.

Later that afternoon, while walking down a local street, we encountered a lady outside her house. We inquired if she was there during the D-Day battle. I have never forgotten her stunning response. She was indeed a resident on D-Day, and heard all the shooting and paratroopers landing, at which time she hid in a fruit preservation cellar and did not come out until daylight. What she saw was dead Germans and some American paratroopers laying around outside her house. It was shocking to her and now, at that moment, to me because being in combat and as soldiers, doing the shooting, we are not concerned as to what the area looks like to a civilian. I could only think of what my kindhearted mother back in Boston would have thought if she ever was in a war area and walked out the next morning to see the bodies of both friendly and enemy soldiers. It was a horrible sight for the French lady and her young daughter, from this very peaceful and quiet town. We never thought about the emotions of the civilians during combat. I learned something that afternoon.

The next day, after inspecting the various battlefields, we visited with the D-Day Mayor, Alexander Reverend, and his wonderful wife Madame (Simone) Renaud. Over coffee and tea we began to talk about the war and how Madame Renaud and the Mayor had dedicated their lives to the memory of the Americans who liberated their town. We agreed we should stay in touch by mail and continue our discussion about helping her to make sure no one forgets what happened in their town as well as all of Normandy, especially our comrades who still buried there.

My close friend, John F. Lee, an 81mm mortar man from Worcester, Massachusetts, and I, told Madame Renaud we were experienced free fall skydivers and we would love to come back on the 20th anniversary of D-Day in 1964 and "drop in" on them. She thought it was a marvelous idea and would be a great effort as a memorial and remembrance to our 82nd Airborne Division soldiers.

We left Ste Mere Eglise and our new friends, the Renaud family, with promises to keep. And we did. John F. Lee and I left Boston for Paris May 30, 1964 with our own parachutes and Madame Renaud's prior assurance she had arranged for a small airplane, pilot and drop zone. All well and good; except President De Gaulle thought we were a couple of American veteran 'nuts' and he had French customs confiscate our parachutes and gear. When Monique La Roche, of Paris, the French woman's skydiving Champion went with us to the airport and told the lone customs agent that Monsieur Murphy and Lee had fought for his freedom and liberation twenty years ago, leaving some of their blood was in French soil, the official tearfully opened the lockup and returned our parachutes.

On 6 June 1964 we went to see Madame Renaud; she had made all the arrangements to make that 20th Anniversary jump, with hundreds of people flocking the field. That second visit in 1964 to Ste Mere Eglise was the beginning of our bond with Madame Renaud, Mayor Renaud (a French WW I combat soldier) and their children, Paul, Henri- Jean and Maurice Renaud, that has lasted to this day. Friendly relations continue with their grandchildren Philippe, Bertrand and Florence, all who have visited with our families in France and America.

I began parachuting with my close friend Yves Tariel, the president of the League D'Amite Parachutiste of France; a practice we continued for some years. We used to jump from French Army C-119 Flying Boxcars into Ste Mere Eglise. We would fly from the Evereux French military base and up the Normandy coast, over the Omaha Beach Cemetery where 3900 of our boys lay buried. We would stand in the aircraft and I salute them from the door as we fly past.

Yves Tariel arranged the annual D-Day jump for many years and it was a great experience to jump with the young French Army paratroopers. My pal Yves Tariel planned and arranged with the military all these jumps for many years, including 1994, the 50th anniversary of D-Day. Thousands of tourists congregate in the town of Ste Mere Eglise, as well as all the other cities and towns and beaches where battles for fought and men died. Veterans from America, Briton, Canada, and other Allied countries, from all different Divisions visit Normandy annually.

We formed the exclusive 'C47 Club' made up of veteran 82nd Airborne Division men who had made a combat jump from a C47 aircraft. We traveled to England, Holland and Belgium to form subsidiary, 'Friends of the 82nd Airborne Division, C47 Club'. The 'Friends' Associations have been going strong for over thirty years, with memorial exercises and friendship visits between the USA, UK, France, Holland and Belgium chapters.

In England, where General Matthew B. Ridgway dedicated a park to the 82nd veterans, we have our friendship club chaired by Deryk Wills who wrote a book about the American 82nd paratroopers and gliderman called "Put On Your Boots And Parachutes", still in print. Deryk and his wife Ann travel frequently to America and, along with their skydiving son David, visited our 505 RCT Association 1999 Reunion at Fort Bragg in October. The U K chapter has it's regular meetings in the Liecester -Oadly area.

In Normandy, each year seems to bring a larger crowd than the year before, with hundreds of re-enactment men, and gals in World War II uniforms, and jeeps, trucks, guns and original WWII equipment of all shapes and sizes. Generally, the 82nd Airborne Division sends a large group of paratroopers who jump over our WW II drop zones. Monsieur Roger Coueffin, the President of the French Association *des Ami Veteran* provides meals and shelter for these paratroopers during their jump-visit. These young troopers don't get on that overseas jump manifest unless they know every fact of the 82nd battles during the 1944 Normandy campaign.

In Ste Mere Eglise there are two museum buildings that you must see during a visit, including a tour inside an original CG4A WACO glider, as well as hundreds of artifacts and photos. In the second building is an original D-Day C47 Aircraft, outfitted and returned to World War II configuration by the French Navy and their Department of Defense. The project was the brain-child of my close French skydiving pal, Yves Tariel, who arranged to get a load of genuine World War II equipment and to have the C47 repainted in the original 1944 colors, including hand painting the black and white stripes around the body of the aircraft. Inside and out, it's all original.

Why do I feel so close to that particular C47? Because I spent about seven years raising money to help with the Ste Mere Eglise building fund. Yves Tariel and I, along with a few other supporting skydivers, made the last jump from that C47 in 1981, before it went inside the museum building forever. It should still be there 300 years from now, along with the documentary accounts of the greatest invasion armada in the history of the world.

Now we came to Holland where we have Father Gerand Thuring, a Catholic priest and pastor of the battle-scarred Saint Antonius church in Groesbeek. Groesbeek, and the surrounding towns were the drop zones of the 504, 505 and 508 para-infantry combat teams along with the 82nd Airborne Division glider troops. It was on a beautiful sunny Sunday afternoon at 1 PM on September 17, 1944 that we defeated the enemy and captured the Nijmegen bridge across the wide Waal River. Tragically, ten miles north the British Airborne lost almost 8000 men at Arnhem, the bridge "Too Far" as Cornelius Ryan's book so detailed that horrible airborne misfortune of the war.

In Groesbeek with the Holland Liberation Committee and its great Museum, Father Thuring and a wonderful Dutch group are dedicated to the memory of the horrors of enemy occupation and their liberation by American and British soldiers. Also, after the 82nd was relieved from combat in this area (and returned to Suippes (Reims), France, the Canadians and British relieved us and took our battle stations and front line positions. Later, in January 1945, they pushed off into Germany after the Battle of the Bulge (Belgium) ended. There are so many good hard working members of this Dutch Association I hesitate to mention all but they deserve much credit for their many years and thousands of hours to memorialize the suffering of their countrymen during the enemy occupation and honor the American Airborne soldiers who liberated them on 17 September 1944. Their prayers were answered that Sunday afternoon and we still visit Pastor Thuring's church for our own prayers and reflection.

If you ever get a chance to go to Belgium at the end of January or in February you will find Emile Lacroix, the foremost leader of the Friends of the 82nd Airborne Division and C47 club Jeep group, leading over 100 veterans and friends in an annual twenty mile march though the cold and snow. Emile has been the chairmen and number one contact person for us in Belgium for twenty-five years. He has never said 'no' to anyone asking for help on a Belgium project.

In fact, Emile Lacroix, of Fernelmont, Belgium, has made all our bronze 505 RCT memorial plaques that are now found in Ste Mere Eglise, Trois Pont and Fosse, Belgium, and in the Groesbeek City Hall (plus several in England). He was an honored guest of the 505 RCT Association at the home of the 82nd Airborne Division at Fort Bragg during October 1999. We can now reflect on the hard work that Emile and the Belgium Friends of the 82nd have done including the annual memorial exercises at the two American cemeteries located in Belgium and their fine museums.

And where did it all start? You will recall when Johnny Lee and I told Madame Renaud in January 1961 at her home behind Alexander Renaud's pharmacy shop "Hey, how about if we "drop in" on you on D-Day 1964". These "Friends of the 82nd -C47 Club" were formed and have remained steadfast over these many years, with closer family friendships, now going onward even with our grandchildren. That was the beginning of these wonderful United Kingdom, French, Holland and Belgium Friendship Associations and, with their absolute dedication, it doesn't look like there is any end in sight.

Robert M. Murphy
Sgt. WW II
Colonel (ret.) Army of the United States

ACKNOWLEDGMENTS
AND SUGGESTIONS FOR RESEARCH

I would like to thank all those 82nd combat soldiers who, over the years, sent me cassette tapes, letters, maps and filled in my la Fiére Manoir and causeway forms. I still have the tape cassettes and forms. The one thing I would like to stress, again, is that no two combat soldiers are likely to agree on what their separate units accomplished or what action was taking place within 100 yards of separate companies. We all did our best. Don't ever be critical of a combat soldier unless you have been in combat and have one or two Purple Hearts.

In the past two years (May 1999) I have had many personal telephone conversations with the men who participated in these battles. After 55 years the memory is hazy but when a group is involved it's surprising how a great event like these battles stirs the memory. At Fort Bragg, N.C., May 20-24, 1997 during the 82nd Airborne Division Annual Review I spoke to men involved, such as Colonel Mark Alexander, Sergeant Jim Blue 508 and my A/505 comrades. By telephone and fax I have communicated with Robert D. Rae, 507, John Marr, 507 and Roy Creek, 507.

Many of the 82nd organic units did not do very well in compiling their history during World War II which is a shame because each man in every unit is entitled to his part of recorded history.

Its a job to write down specific details but it can be done through reliable testimony and comparison of one detail as against another. Some authors really never took the time to do that. Most copied one mistake after another or relied on "tall stories".

If a reader deserves to go to the books I suggest you start with the U. S. Army History with plenty of maps of the battle areas and daily movements of the Normandy battle in "Utah Beach to Cherbourg." Of course one will want the Omaha Beach story. Next for daily general notations but not in specific detail see "82nd Airborne Division, Operation Neptune, Normandy 6 June to 8 July 1944." That WW II booklet had details that include the tail numbers of every Glider that landed in Normandy, what it was carrying and whether or not it was damaged or its men were killed on landing.

A serious student may refer to the 505 World War II history written by Allen Langdon of Company C/505. Langdon was wounded at la Fiére on 6 June by an artillery blast. That history refutes some of what Colonel S. L. A. Marshall had to say in his history of the Normandy battles by the 82nd and 101st Airborne Division. In fact, Allen said that Marshall took a lot of "literary license" in writing his narrative historical documentary one month after the battles in July 1944. However, let us remember if it were not for S.L.A. Marshall and his entire historical team interviewing men within 30 days of their return to England, we would have practically no day by day description by the front line infantrymen.

Marshall didn't mince words. Later, he wrote a book called "Night Drop" about the D-Day Airborne (82-101) battles, published by Little - Brown Co., Boston. It is, in some places, almost word for word taken from his July and August 1944 Historical Section Reports. It contains details of the A/505 two day battle at la Fiére and Lieutenant John (Red Dog) Dolan's "No Better Place To Die" chapter.

The 508 has a good book put together by Don Jakeway who went "all the way" with H Company 508 and has returned many times to Ste. Mere Eglise, Holland and his battle grounds in the Ardennes and Germany. It's filled with personal stories by many men.

General Gavin's book "On to Berlin" is a story of his World War II battles and personal involvement in each campaign from Sicily to Berlin. In many cases he doesn't elaborate on exactly what part he played in the battle but I can assure you he was up front and as close to the enemy as any front line soldier. In fact, after being in Holland for two weeks and in a front line outpost (nobody out front but the enemy), along comes a jeep from the German lines. I took aim to spray the jeep with a BAR and luckily I held my fire. It was General Jim Gavin and a driver in the jeep. He said to me, "I didn't see any Germans from where I came from and, oh, by the way, thanks for holding up on firing." We would go to the wall and over a cliff for that man, one of the best generals in WW II.

The U. S. Army Archives in Washington D.C., Carlisle Barracks in Pennsylvania, Army Museums such as the 82nd Airborne Museum at Fort Bragg (a great one) have thousands of documents, photos and histories. The problem is that it take a serious historian hundreds of hours before he can ever begin to start a detailed documentary or report. Those who have never written or spent any time in writing about history should be grateful for the authors who took the time to write about the famous battles, even though they may have made a few factual mistakes here and there.

There are a few Normandy accounts regarding the 505 but the official battle report, day by day and hour by hour was kept by my very good friend (and namesake) Captain Robert Martin Piper, (Colonel, retired, U. S. Army) Adjutant 505, during the Normandy campaign. It also had every 505 paratrooper KIA in the battle.

I very much desire to thank the *Association Des Ami Veteran Americain*, called the AVA, and its President Roger Coueffin as well as its entire staff and membership for taking care of the returning D-Day airborne veterans and their families for thirty years. This AVA was founded by Madame Simone Renaud, and her husband the D-Day Mayor, Alexandre Renaud. The AVA has formed everlasting memories with hundreds of veterans with visits between countries and homes. Indeed, my children and my 18 year old grandson Ryan Murphy, are friends of the Renaud, Coueffin and Gabriel Roales families.

At the time of this writing I am soon off to what may be the last reunion at Normandy for many of us. Quite an affair is planned and the author will have the pleasure of dedicating a new plaque on the 'Iron Mike' statue at la Fiére. At 0900 on June 5, 1999 there will a ceremony at la Fiére, followed by a parachute jump there at 1400h. Cermonies at Chef-du-Pont, Picauville, Ste. Mere Eglise and the cemeteries and the airborne cemetery will be followed by mass at the local church on June 5-6.

APPENDIX A
Sgt. Bill Owens and Bob Murphy

MEMORIES regarding friendship of Sergeant William D. Owens and Sergeant (Colonel, ret.) Robert M. Murphy. Bill Owens was approximately 37 years old when Bob Murphy, age 17, came into "A" Company 505, First Platoon in Africa. Owens treated Murphy like a son because of their large age spread. They dug in and fought together in Italy and bunked in the same tent in England, along with co-radio men and runner Darrell Franks; who was a practical joker. During mid May (1944) after a long hot day of training exercises Owens sat down by a tree, took off his heavy helmet and put on his field overseas cap. He was shy because of going bald. Murphy, at Frank's coaching, cut the long hair off a horse in the field and tucked it under the cap of the now sleeping Sergeant Owens. The loud laughter on the squad caused Owens to wake. He saw the horses hair over his eyes and sleepily imagined it as his own hair until he saw the squad rolling in laughter, pointing the finger at Bob Murphy. Fortunately, he could take a joke and it was a jovial relaxation spell for the co-conspirator squad and platoon members.

On another occasion, only a little more serious, after our Holland combat jump on 17 September 1944, Billy Owens and Bob Murphy got stuck behind German lines on patrol one night and the entire next day. On return to a tiny 4 x 4 x 4 preserve cellar in a house while sitting with our backs to the wall and legs spread we were having a snack and cleaning our weapons, Bill Owens by error discharged his .45 pistol, after putting a round in the chamber, and the bullet ricocheted off the cement floor into Murphy's jacket and stomach. Owen's turned white. Murphy reached in to feel for the blood but pulled out the .45 round which bounced off his German "Gott Mitt Uns" metal belt buckle Murphy wore with his German P38 pistol. Owens never forgot that misfire and in June of 1964 he wrote to Bob Murphy about that incident (and others). After Murphy's 20th anniversary parachute jump into Ste. Mere Eglise on 6 June 1964 and a news article about that jump they corresponded and spoke frequently until Owens death.

APPENDIX B
Wayne Pierce - 1st Lieutenant, 1/325 Glider Infantry on Recollection of Normandy, June 9, 1944

The afternoon of June 8, 1944 Major Teddy Sanford, C.O. 1st Battalion, 325 Glider Infantry Regiment, on orders from Col. Lewis and BG Gavin, made plans to cross the Merderet River and attack the Germans holding the West bank of the river at the la Fiére Cauquigny Church causeway. We were to be led across the ford by a 507 Lieutenant who had come across the ford seeking assistance for a group of 507 men under the command of Lt. Colonel Timmes. These 100 or so men under Timmes had been holed up at a farm and orchard, now known as the Jules Jean farm, since landing on D-Day.

Contrary to the report of some historians about this action, Sanford's attack order was issued before darkness on June 8th and was not altered after the maneuver got underway.

Teddy Sanford's plan of attack was that we proceed in a column of companies in the order of Company C, A and B. Company C was to ford the river and turn slightly to the right and attack what we called the "gray castle" where German troops were known to be entrenched. Company C was to make a show of firepower against the "gray castle", then fall back to the farm orchard.

Company "A", next in line was to proceed through the orchard, turn to the left and follow a country lane about one half mile to a road junction near le Motey. Here they were to set up a blocking action to keep German reinforcements from the la Fiére-Cauquigny causeway and protect the rear of the attacking force.

Company B, next in line would pass through the orchard then turn almost 180 degrees to the left, attack toward the Cauquigny Church, guiding on the road on their right flank. After falling back from the "gray castle", Company C was to align on the right of Company B in the attack toward the causeway.

The battalion forded the river a little after midnight. Company C made their feint toward the gray castle and fell back in line for the attack. Although it was a dark night, companies B and C moved out in attack formation with good control.

Major Sanford and I, along with about four or five men, (runners, telephone and radio communication men) followed the left platoon of Company C to try to be as near the center of the attacking force as possible. We crossed the road leading from Cauquigny to le Motey and proceeded over a slight rise through a wheat field.

In the darkness, Company C and B lost contact and Company C drifted slightly to the right from the road on their left intended as a guiding terrain feature. Although the time was almost 4 a.m. it was still very dark.

As company C reached the end of the wheat field and entered an orchard, sporadic firing commenced. The company moved rapidly through the orchard until they reached a sunken road. We picked up one German prisoner in our C.P. group.

Firing in the sunken road became very intense, then would become silent. German voices could be heard. The platoon our C.P. group was following were completely committed in or beyond the sunken road. Our C. P. group was probably 30 or so yards back along the hedgerow in the orchard. Major Sanford inched forward during one of the lulls in the firing and almost became embroiled in the fire-fight, throwing a grenade, then trying to determine the situation. As dawn began to streak the morning sky, Sanford could see and hear only Germans.

He crawled back to where I was hugging the ground and whispered that it looked like Company C was "wiped out". He told our C. P. group to start retracing our path back to the orchard where the 507 men were holding out.

By this time it was rapidly becoming daylight. The CP group moved back, I squatted on my haunches, not having looked down into the sunken road, I was not sure that it was time to move back. Looking back I could now see Sanford and the CP group along with the German POW topping the rise in the wheat field. Looking around me I saw that I was in a German artillery position. A large howitzer loomed over me but I seemed to be completely alone.

To try to determine for myself what was going on, I ran past the German howitzer, across the orchard to the hedgerow on the opposite side. Here I peered through the hedge and saw no living person. The activity in the sunken road and beyond began to grow louder. A vehicle was moving up the road from Cauquigny, perhaps a small tank. German voices could be heard but no sign of an American. At this point, I was as convinced as Sanford that Company C had been "wiped out."

I moved out at a fast pace, through the wheat field and there after topping the rise in the ground, I found six or eight Company C men. They believed, correctly, that their company had been decimated and that some of the men had surrendered. They told of a German officer who tried to get them to surrender but they had gotten away. While I returned to the orchard, I had about 20 men from Company C with me.

Personal Comments:

The 325 Glider Infantry prior to and through Normandy was "light infantry." Each rifle company in this attack had only two rifle platoons, there was no maneuvering reserve force that could be held back. In this situation, Company "A", located in a blocking action, was not free to come forward to help extricate Company C. A rifle company at full strength had 150 men. The companies of the 1st Battalion in this attack probably had less than 120 men each.

Sanford and I were undoubtedly following the platoon with DeGlopper assigned as a BAR man. The fire-fight in the sunken road and beyond was extremely fierce. There is no question, Company C was out-numbered and out gunned in this fight. The platoon leader, Lt. Johnson, was K.I.A.

Lt Kinsey leading the Company C right flank platoon was awarded the DSC for his action in this attack. He too was wounded and captured but while in a German hospital, took a sleeping guard's pistol and escaped back to the American lines. Kinsey's wounds were so severe that he was returned to the States. (Kinsey is deceased)

Major Sanford when ordered to make this night attack was told the Germans holding the bridgehead were estimated to be no more than one company reinforced with automatic weapons and possibly two light tanks. If this had been true, Sanford believed the attack would have been a "pushover."

Ridgway and Gavin did not alter their estimate of the German strength when they ordered the 3rd Battalion of the 325 to attack across the causeway the morning of June 9th. After that battle, Gavin admitted that he had not realized the strength of the German force at Cauquigny.

Further comments about the action of DeGlopper would be hearsay on my part. The darkness and the heavy hedges surrounding the orchard and along the sunken road made it impossible for me to be an eye witness to the action from my location.

𝕬𝖗𝖙𝖍𝖚𝖗 𝕯.𝕷𝖎𝖙𝖙𝖑𝖊,𝕴𝖓𝖈.

ESTABLISHED 1886

THIRTY MEMORIAL DRIVE
CAMBRIDGE 42, MASSACHUSETTS

UNIVERSITY
4-5770

March 27, 1959

Mr. Cornelius Ryan
230 East Forty-eighth Street
New York 17, New York

Dear Connie:

I just received the attached from Dolan. Frankly,
it is the first time that I have ever gotten this
much detail out of him. Although I was with him
from beginning to end of the War, he was never much
for talking about what happened. I hasten to send
it off to you because I think that it is quite good.
To the best of my knowledge it is accurate in every
detail.

Sincerely

James M. Gavin
Executive Vice President

mhm

Enclosures (7)

Appendix 5. Captain John J. Dolan's March 23, 1959 seven page letter to General James M. Gavin (written at the urging of Robert Attorney Robert M. Murphy)

CAMBRIDGE, MASS.   NEW YORK   CHICAGO   WASHINGTON, D.C.   SAN FRANCISCO   SCOTLAND   PUERTO RICO

CHINOWTH AND COMPANY
Reinforcing Steel Contractors
101 La Entrada Pl.
Fullerton, California
Phone AN 2-6141
March 16th, 1959

William D.Owens
10409 E.Olive St.
Temple City,Calif.

General J.M.Gavin
Acorn Park
Cambridge &0,Mass.

Dear Sir;

Thank you for your letter of March the 9th,I do like to
hear from you now and again. I see that Mr Ryan has been
in touch with you regarding the questionnaire I filled out
and sent to him.

I am inclosing my story concerning The 1st Platoons action
on June 6th,7th and 8th.I sincerely hope that it will help
him. I wish you to read it and see if it is alright. For the
life of me I cant recall the 1st Battalion commander at that
time but believe it was Miller any way I am sure you will have
the record of him and know his name. I know that he will not
use most of it but I wanted to say everything that happened
to us,I hope that I didnt include my own action too much but
I think it better this way and as I said,he canduse what he
wants.

Thank you again for all your efforts in my behalf regarding
the C.M.H. I am realy sorry that I didnt receive it for it
would have pleased my Family and some of the men.

If I can ever be of service to you in any way,please call on
me. As you can see I8m not an expert on this Typewritter but
know that he will write it again .

With Kindest regards

Bill Owens

Bill Owens

APPENDIX E
Marcus Heim's (DSC) story - D-Day June 6, 1944

A little after midnight On June 6, 1944 I jumped out of a C-47 aircraft over Normandy with the 82nd Airborne. Our objective was the crossroads of the town of Ste. Mere Eglise and the Merderet and Dove River valleys. I was with "A" Company, 505 PIR and our objective was the la Fiére bridge over the Merderet.

I landed about twenty-five feet from a road before I could get my rifle assembled. I heard a motorcycle approaching and remained still and watched two German soldiers pass by. After they passed and I assembled my firearm I found other paratroopers and our equipment bundle and set off for the bridge at la Fiére. We were to hold the bridge until the soldiers who landed on the beach arrived later on D-Day, but it was three days before they reached our position.

As you stand at the la Fiére bridge looking in the direction of Ste. Mere Eglise the Manoir house is on the right. There are several buildings, one a large barn which was close to the Merderet. The Germans had occupied the Manoir and were driven out by A/505 after heavy fighting. As you pass the Manoir towards Ste. Mere Eglise the road goes up a hill and curves to the left. Across from the Manoir there was a pathway which was about four feet wide and is now a paved road some seven feet wide. As you look across the bridge towards Cauquigny, the causeway was narrow and had brush and trees on each side, some creating a canopy over the causeway. The fields were completely flooded right up to the causeway. The village of Cauquigny lies about 800 yards from the bridge, and it was in German hands. The causeway curved to the right about 65 yards from the bridge.

When we arrived at the bridge, men were placed down the pathway to the right and left of the Manoir and out-buildings. The four bazooka-men, Lenold Peterson, myself, John Bolderson and Gordon Pryne were given our positions. We (Peterson and Heim) were deployed on the Manoir side facing Cauquigny, below the driveway. There was a telephone pole just in front of us and we dug in behind it. We (Peterson and Heim) knew that when the Germans started the attack with their tanks we would have to get out of our foxhole and reveal our position so we could get a better view of the tanks. Bolderson and Pryne were on the right side of the road just below the pathway. I do not remember how many paratroopers were around, all I saw was a machine-gun set up in the manor house yard. On the right side down the pathway a few riflemen were placed. There was a 57mm gun up the road in back of us along with another machine-gun. We carried anti-tank mines and bazooka rockets from the landing area. These mines were placed across the causeway about 50 feet on the other side of the bridge. There was a broken-down German truck by the manor house which we pushed and dragged across the bridge and placed across the causeway. All that afternoon the Germans kept shelling our positions and the rumor was that the Germans were going to counter-attack. Around 5:00 P.M. the enemy started to attack. Two tanks with infantry on each side and in the rear following them was a third tank with more infantry following it. As the lead tank started around the curve in the road the tank commander stood up in the turret to take a look and from our left the machine-gun let loose a burst and killed the commander. At the same time the bazookas, 75 millimeter gun and anything else we had fired at the Germans and they in turn were shooting at us with cannons, mortars, machine-gun and rifle fire. Lenold Peterson, the gunner and myself (Heim), the loader, in the forward position got out of our foxhole and stood behind the telephone pole so we could get a better shot at the tank. We had to hold our fire until the last minute because some of the tree branches along the causeway were blocking our view. The first tank was hit and started to turn sideways and at the same time it was swinging its turret around and firing at us. We (Peterson and Heim) had just moved forward around the cement telephone pole when a German round hit it and we had to jump out of the way to avoid being hit as it was falling. I was hoping that Bolderson and Pryne were also firing at the tanks for with all that was happening in front of us there was no time to see what others were doing. We (Peterson and Heim) kept firing at the first tanks until it was put out of action and on fire. The second tank came up and pushed the first tank out of the way. We moved forward toward the second tank and fired at it as fast as I could load the rockets into the bazooka. We kept firing at the second tank and we hit it in the turret where the body joins it, also in the tracks and with another hit it also went up in flames. We (Peterson and Heim) were almost out of rockets and the third tank was still moving. Peterson asked me to go back and across the road to see if Bolderson had any extra rockets. I ran across the road and with all the cross-fire I still find it hard to believe I made it across in one piece. When I got to the other side I found one dead soldier by Bolderson and Pryne were gone. Their bazooka was lying on the ground and it was damaged by what I thought were bullet holes. Not finding Bolderson or Pryne I presumed that either one or both of them were injured. I found the rockets they left and then had to return across the road to where I left Peterson. The Germans were still firing at us and I was lucky again. I returned without being hit. Peterson and myself with the new rockets put these to use against the third tank. After that one was put out of action the Germans pulled back to Cauquigny and continued shelling us for the rest of the night. They also tried two other attacks on our positions.

Our job was to be in the forward position with our bazooka and stop the Germans from using the la Fiére bridge. This we accomplished despite the tremendous and continual firing by the enemy. When the Germans retreated, Peterson and myself were still in our positions at the bridge and as we looked around we could not see anyone so we moved back to our foxhole. Looking back up the hill we could see that the 57 millimeter gun and our machine-gun had been destroyed. Then someone came and told us to should our position and that more men would be coming to take up other positions. We found later that of the few men holding the bridge most were either killed or wounded.

This was one of the toughest days of my life. Why we (Peterson and Heim) were not injured or killed, only the Good Lord knows.

APPENDIX F
Charles DeGlopper's Medal of Honor Citation

RANK AND ORGANIZATION: Private First Class, Co. C. 325th Glider Infantry, 82nd Airborne Division. PLACE AND DATE: Merderet River at La Fiere, France, 9 June 1944. ENTERED SERVICE AT: Grand Island, N.Y. BIRTH: Grand Island, N.Y. G.O. No.: 22, 28 Feb. 1946. CITATION: He was a member of Company C, 325th Glider Infantry, on 9 June 1944 advancing with the forward platoon to secure a bridgehead across the Merderet River at La Fiere, France. At dawn the platoon had penetrated an outer line of machine guns and riflemen, but in so doing had become cut off from the rest of the company. Vastly superior forces began a decimation of the stricken unit and put in motion a flanking maneuver which would have completely exposed the American platoon in a shallow roadside ditch where it had taken cover. Detecting this danger, Private DeGlopper volunteered to support his comrades by fire from his automatic rifle while they attempted a withdrawal through a break in a hedgerow 40 yards to the rear. Scorning a concentration of enemy automatic weapons and rifle fire, he walked from the ditch onto the road in full view of the Germans, and sprayed the hostile positions with assault fire. He was wounded, but he continued firing. Struck again, he started to fall; and yet his grim determination and valiant fighting spirit could not be broken. Kneeling in the roadway, weakened by his grievous wounds, he leveled his heavy weapon against the enemy and fired burst after burst until killed outright. He was successful in drawing the enemy action away from his fellow soldiers, who continued the fight from a more advantageous position and established the first bridgehead over the Merderet. In the area where he made his intrepid stand his comrades later found the ground strewn with dead Germans and many machine guns and automatic weapons which had knocked out of action. Private DeGlopper's gallant sacrifice and unflinching heroism while facing insurmountable odds were in great measure responsible for a highly important tactical victory in the Normandy Campaign.

Charles DeGlopper, C/325 Congressional Medal of Honor winner.

94

ARTHUR J. MARTIN
JOSEPH W. BREEN
JOHN F. DAVIS

TELEPHONE HANCOCK 6- {6630
6662

JOHN J. DOLAN
ATTORNEY AT LAW
BOX 1272, 141 MILK STREET
BOSTON 4, MASS.

March 23, 1959

Lt. General James M. Gavin
c/o Arthur D. Little, Inc.
30 Memorial Drive
Cambridge, Mass.

Dear General Gavin:

Thank you for your letter of March 10, 1959. It had always
been my intention of answering the questionnaire of Cornelius Ryan;
but realizing that it would take considerable time to give a detailed
and accurate account, I kept putting it aside and then completely
forgot about it until Bob Murphy spoke to me about it a few days before
receipt of your letter.

I shall try to cover as much detail without making this letter
too voluminous, leaving it to your judgment and discretion to delete
any portion that you deem unfavorable to the outfit.

You may recall that I was in command of Company "A", 505
Prcht.Infantry, with the rank of First Lieutenant. The specific mission
of the Company "A" was to seize and defend the bridge crossing the
Merderet River on the road that ran East to West from Ste. Mere Eglise,
with the purpose of preventing the movement of German troops down to
the beach-head.

I don't recall exactly what time the first Batallion jumped,
but it was between 1:00 and 2:00 a.m. on "D" Day. We hit our drop zone
right on the nose, because within twenty minutes to one-half hour, I
knew our exact location. I was able to identify a "T" intersection,
dirt roads 8 to 10 feet wide, near our drop zone. The upper arm of which
ran generally east to west, the vertical arm running north to south, to
meet the road running from Ste. Mere Eglise to our objective, the
bridge at the Merderet River.

We had the usual problems of re-organization in the dark; however,
about an hour before dawn, Company "A" moved out from the drop zone with
about ninety (90) per cent of the men accounted for. (This was not
due to luck alone, but to the cooperation of my Officers, Non-Coms, and
last but not least, training. Men who have to fight in the night should

be trained in night-time fighting, not just taken on a night march and
digging fox holes.) We moved along this dirt road which I previously
referred to as being the North-South arm of the "T" intersection, and
just around here, I ran into Major McGinity. He moved out with us.

The order of March was first, Co. Headquarters, third and
second platoons in that order. When we reached the road running East-
West from Ste. Mere Eglise, a German motorcycle passed us going toward
Ste. Mere Eglise. At this time, it was still dark, but daylight was
starting to break. We crossed the road and started west toward the
bridge, with a hedge row to our right between us and the road. Just
about this time, contact was lost with the first platoon, so the third
platoon took the lead.

About seven to eight hundred yards from the bridge, we came
upon a dirt road running southeasterly from the road to the bridge.
Hedge rows were on either side of this road; and beyond it in the
direction of the bridge, was an open, flat field, about 100 yards deep,
and about 75 yards wide. It was here that I figured the Germans would
defend if they intended a defense of the bridge.

I directed Lt. Donald Coxon to send his scouts out. This he
did, and he also went out with them. He had plenty of personal courage
but he didn't have the heart to order them out without going with them.

A few moments later, a German machine gun opened up, killing
Lt. Coxon and one of his scouts, Ferguson. Their fire was returned; and,
with Major McGinity and myself leading, a few men holding and returning
frontal fire, the platoon flanked to the left. At the same time, I
directed Lt. Presnell to re-cross the road and attack along the northerly
side down to the bridge. This was done, and the second platoon didn't
meet with any fire until they arrived at the bridge.

The third platoon continued its flanking move and cut back in
toward the road to the bridge. Because of the fire, we calculated that
there was just one machine gun crew that was in our way. It later turned
out that there must have been at least a squad dug in at this point,
with at least two of them armed with machine pistols. Prisoners
captured later, in addition to the German dead, amounted to about the
size of one of our platoons. There were no German officers captured.
I don't know whether or not any of their enlisted men escaped.

To continue, we cut back toward the road, travelling in a
Northerly direction. Major McGinity was leading and I was about three
or four paces behind, and slightly to the right. There was a high,
thick hedge row to our left, and it was in here that I figured the machine
gun was located.

When we had travelled about two-thirds of the way up the hedge row, they opened up on us with rifle fire, and at least two machine pistols. I returned the fire with my Thompson Sub-Machine Gun at a point where I could see leaves in the hedge row fluttering. Major McGinity was killed instantly. As luck would have it, there was a German foxhole to my left, which I jumped into and from where I continued to fire. I could only guess where to shoot, but I had to, as part of the Third platoon was exposed to their fire. Lt. McLaughlin, the assistant platoon leader was wounded and died later that day. His radio operator was also killed. The platoon by now was under fire from two directions, from the point where I was pinned down, and also from the direction of the bridge.

I can't estimate how long we were pinned down in this fashion, but it was at least an hour. I made several attempts to move, but drew their fire. On my last attempt, I drew no fire. They obviously had pulled out.

During all of this time, I could hear rifle and machine gun fire down by the bridge on the north side. This ceased about this time. I returned to the rest of the third platoon, instructed the Non-Coms to re-organize and to maintain their present position. I then crossed the road and located the first platoon commanded by Lt. Oakley on the north side. They were moving toward the bridge, so I instructed them to continue and dig in on the right side. I went down to the bridge and found that we had received an assist from some of the 508 Prcht. Infantry. About this time, I ran into Col. Eckman, and sent for my third platoon to dig in on the left or south side of the bridge. The first was already digging in on the north side.

I thought that all of the Germans had retreated; but unknown to us, there were about ten or twelve Germans holed up on the second floor of a stucco-type farm house. At the time they started firing, Col. Eckman and I were casually looking the situation over. It lasted about twenty minutes with about ten or twelve Germans surrendering. About a squad of men from the 508 made the actual capture.

We dug in, the disposition of my Company as follows: First platoon on the north side of the road, the third on the south and the second in reserve, about 400 yards back, so that it could also protect the rear.

Major Kellam arrived at the bridge with Capt. Roysden, his S-3. He had most of his C.P. unit with him. I don't know whether or not a Batallion C.P. had ever been set up as planned, at least, I don't recall having had any communication with it. Down at the bridge now was most of Company "A", about one platoon of Company "B", a platoon of the Division Engineers (mission to blow the bridge if necessary), about half of Batallion Headquarters Company with mortars and machine gun sections and several stray men from other regiments.

The Company dug in well and quickly. I had just completed my inspection of the forward positions when we knew that an attack was coming. You will recall that in front of our position, west of the Merderet River, was a marsh at least 1000 yards wide at its narrowest point. The road running west from the bridge could better be described as a causway.

As I recall, the mission of the 508 was to occupy a position beyond this causway. In addition to the men who assisted us in capturing the bridge at least a company of the 508 passed through our position and moved over the causway to their objective. They were gone at least an hour when we saw several of them retreating back across the marsh. I remember that we helped several of them out of the river, which was quite shallow.

The machine gun fire from the Germans was very heavy by now. We didn't return their fire as there were no visible targets and our ammunition supply was limited. They attacked with three tanks, which I was unable to identify for sure; but they appeared to be similar to the German Mark IV type, or maybe a little lighter. The tanks were firing on us with machine guns and cannon.

Just about a half-hour before this attack, a 57MM A. T. gun was assigned to Company "A". I located this gun about 150 yards from the bridge on the road where it curves to the right as you approach the bridge. Incidentally, this was my C.P. and later the Batallion C.P. This gave the gun excellent cover and a good field of fire.

On the bridge I had three bazooka teams. Two of them were from Company "A" and the third was either from "B", or "C" Company. The two Company "A" bazookas were dug in to the left and right of the bridge. Because of the fact that the road itself was the causeway type, they were as of necessity dug in below the level of the road, so that in order to fire, they had to get out of their fox holes. The third bazooka was over more to the south where better cover was available.

To continue, I had just completed my inspection of our defenses and was 40 to 50 yards from the bridge. Major Kellam and Captain Roysden were nearby.

The first two tanks were within 15 or 20 yards of each other, the third was back about 50 yards. When the lead tank was about 40 or 50 yards away from the bridge, the two Company "A" bazooka teams

got up just like clock work to the edge of the road. They were under
the heaviest small arms fire from the other side of the causeway, and
from the cannon and machine gun fire from the tanks. To this day, I'll
never be able to explain why all four of them were not killed. They
fired and reloaded with the precision of well oiled machinery. Watching
them made it hard to believe that this was nothing but a routine drill.
I don't think that either crew wasted a shot. The first tank received
several direct hits. The treads were knocked off, and within a matter
of minutes it was on fire.

Then they went to work on the second tank, and within about
30 seconds, it was on fire. They fired every rocket that they had and
then jumped into their foxholes. The 57MM during this time was firing
and eventually knocked out the last tank. The gun crew did an excellent
job.

My two bazooka crews called for more ammunition. Major Kellam
ran up toward the bridge with a bag of rockets followed by Captain Roysden.
When they were within 15 or 20 yards of the bridge, the Germans opened
up with mortar fire on the bridge. Major Kellam was killed and Captain
Roysden was rendered unconscious from the concussion. He died later
that day.

Both of the bazookas were destroyed by the mortar fire.
Lt. Weir (Reg. Hq. Co.) and I carried Captain Roysden back. I then took
over command of the batallion, being the senior officer present.

Company "B" was put into reserve in the perimeter of Company "A",
so that we had almost a 360 degree perimeter defense. The rest of the
day we were under heavy mortar and machine gun fire. The mortar fire
was very effective as against the two forward platoons because of tree
bursts. It took very little imagination on the part of the Krauts to
figure out just where we would be dug in. As I recall, there was less
than a seventy-five yard frontage on either side of the bridge from
where we could effectively defend, so they could throw their mortar fire
in our general direction with good results. During the night, the fire
let up, but they started early the next morning and kept it up. My
third platoon took the worst beating, as they were in a heavily wooded
area, (tree bursts).

The second tank attack came on the afternoon of the second day.
I was over on the north side of the bridge with the first platoon. For
about an hour before the attack, they increased their mortar fire to the
extent that the third platoon was just about knocked out, but not quite.
I was not aware of this at the time. In addition to already heavy
casualties, Sgt. Monahan, the platoon Sgt. was fatally wounded.

I learned second hand that some other troops had retreated through the third platoon's position, and then through my C.P. Rumors were around that we were going to give up the bridge. As a result of this, the 57MM A.T. crew took off. I didn't have an Executive Officer at the time. Earlier that day, he (Tom Furey) was put in command of Company "C". My First Sargeant was a jump casualty, so my Company Headquarters at the time was non-existent except for runners and radio operators. I can't recall why, but our radios were not working. The only way that we could communicate was through runners.

The first platoon was under heavy fire also. The platoon leader, Lt. Oakley, who had been doing an excellent job, was fatally wounded, and Sgt. Ricci was   leaving the junior squad leader, Sgt. Owens, in command. You will recall that we have had some communication about Sgt. Owens in the past as to his personal courage and the way he commanded the platoon at this most critical time.

I recommended Sgt. Owens and my four bazooka men for the D.S.C. The bazooka men were awarded the D.S.C., but Sgt. Owens was not. This is a story in itself.

The second attack was with two tanks and infantry. I was unable to estimate the size. The tanks stayed out of effective bazooka range. (We had one bazooka left.) Not hearing any fire from the 57MM, I went over to it and found it unmanned. I tried to fire it, but the crew had taken the firing mechanism. I organized five or six men behind the hedge on the southerly side of the road with Gammon grenades, and just about this time, two of the gun crew returned with the firing mechanism. They knocked out the two tanks. They were two youngsters not more than 17 or 18 years old, who returned on their own initiative. I recommended them for Silver Stars.

The rest of our stay at the bridge was uneventful, except for the continued mortar fire, and at the end, artillery fire which damaged the 57MM.

Lt. Col. Mark Alexander took over command of the batallion later that day and continued to command it for most of the operation. Without exception, he was the finest battalion commander I ever served under. My second son, Mark Alexander Dolan, was named after him.

In conclusion, we held the bridge until relieved. In Co. "A" alone, in those days (three in all), we had seventeen known dead and about three times that number wounded. The rest of the batallion also had heavy casualties.

I have tried to give you an accurate picture of what happened; however, after fifteen years, the foregoing may contain some minor inaccuracies.

I will be glad to give Mr. Ryan any additional information he may require. You may assure him that I will be happy to cooperate with him in every detail.

Very truly yours,

JJD:eg

John J. Dolan

P.S.   Since writing this letter, I have read the account by David Howarth in the Saturday Evening Post, and I agree with you that it contains many inaccuracies. You will probably note that some of the events related tie in with what I have told you in this letter.

The most glaring inaccuracy is about the bridge being lost. For the record, this bridge was held by Company "A" from the time of its capture on "D" Day, until we were relieved.

There are a few other incidents that happened down at the bridge, which I will relate to you, as it is my intention to drop in on you at some time within the next few weeks.

APPENDIX H
German Army Report Dated June 6, 1944

X - 567

Carentan is in our hands. Near Ste. Marie du Mont still
enemy forces. Near La Madeleine the enemy has a foothold.
From there to the north our troops are holding firm.
The report that St. Vaast is taken by the enemy has not
been confirmed.

The parachute troops that jumped into the area Ste. Mère-
Église are attacking toward the east.

The 91st Air Borne Division (German, T.) is in battle
there. No details yet.

1330   <u>Report Navy Liaison Officer</u>:
As of 1225 Naval Commander Seine-Somme reports: According
to report from signal station Cap de la Heve observed:
5 battle ships, 15 light and heavy cruisers, about 50
destroyers and Torpedo Boats, 12 troop transports, 25
Tank Landing Ships and innumerable landing craft.
The force is continually growing. In the background
there are still many ships that can not be made out.

1645   <u>Air Warning Center reports</u>:
1636 several planes circling in area Gisors (sic) -
Mantes.

<u>Air Force Liaison reports</u>:

1245 - 1345: 6 fighter formations; 83 fighters
reported in area Caen, Laigle, Chartres, Reims, Valencien-
nes, Dunkirk,
Bombing south of Rambouillet and west of Paris.

Since 1020 - 1410: four-engine formations with strong
fighter protection in area Le Havre and east of Alençon,
west of Flers. Bombings area Caen, south of Alençon,
and in area Cherbourg.

Since 1410 - 1600: Continuous flights of fighter formations
into area Somme estuary, Creil, west of Paris, Dreux,
Le Mans, Angers, Rennes, St. Malo. Some fighter formations

-10-

The Parachutist's Creed

I volunteered as a parachutist, fully realizing the hazards of my chosen service; and by my thoughts and by my actions will always uphold the prestige, honor, and rich esprit-de-corps of the only volunteer branch of the Army.

I realize that a parachutist is not merely a soldier who arrives by parachute to fight, but an elite shocktrooper, and that his country expects him to march further and faster, to fight harder, to be more self reliant and to soldier better than any other soldier. Parachutists of all allied armies belong to this great brotherhood.

I shall never fail my fellow comrades by shirking any duty or training, but will always keep myself mentally and physically fit and shoulder my full share of the task, whatever it may be.

I shall always accord my superiors my fullest loyalty and I will always bear in mind the sacred trust I have in the lives of the men I lead into battle.

I shall show other soldiers, by military courtesy to my superior officers and noncommissioned officers, by my neatness in dress, by my care for my weapons and equipment, that I am a picked and well trained soldier.

I shall endeavor by my soldierly appearance, military bearing and behavior, to reflect the high standards of training and morale of parachute troops.

I shall respect the abilities of my enemies, I will fight fairly and with all my might. SURRENDER IS NOT IN MY CREED.

I shall display a higher degree of initiative than is required of the other troops and will fight on to my objective and mission, though I be the lone survivor.

I will prove my ability as a fighting man against the enemy on the field of battle, not by quarreling with my comrades in arms or by bragging about my deeds, thus needlessly arousing jealousy and resentment against parachute troops.

I shall always realize that battles are won by an army fighting as a team, that I fight and blaze a path into battle for others to follow and carry the battle on.

I belong to the finest unit in the army. By my appearance, actions, and battlefield deeds alone, I speak for my fighting ability. I will strive to uphold the honor and prestige of my outfit, making my country proud of me and of the unit to which I belong.

APPENDIX J
82nd AB Historical Notes

82nd AIRBORNE DIVISION

The division was activated during WW I and nicknamed the "All American" because it had members from all 48 states. It spent more days in the front than any other American division and was the home of such heroes as Alvin York and Jonathan Wainwright. After WW I, the division was inactivated.

1942: The 82nd Infantry Division, reactivated under the command of MG Omar Bradley. Division reorganized and redesignated as the Army's first Airborne Division. Moved to Fort Bragg, under the command of MG Matthew Ridgway to train for parachute and glider operations.

1943: April, the 82nd began deployment to North Africa for airborne assaults into Sicily. July, the 505 and 504 Combat Teams made parachute assaults against German and Italian forces - the first major combat jumps of an American division. September, the 504 and 505 Combat Teams jumped into the Allied beachheads at Salerno, Italy. This airborne reinforcement saved the US 5th Army's foothold in Italy. November, the division (less the 504) embarked for the United Kingdom to begin training for the invasion of Normandy.

1944: January, the 504 Combat Team participated in assault landings at Anzio in Italy. The 504 would rejoin the division in April.
6 June, the 82nd using parachutes and gliders made a combat assault against German forces in Normandy. Thirty-three days of unrelenting combat followed, bringing great battle honors to the division, as well as a 49% casualty rate. 17 September, the 82nd landed in Holland, some 50 miles behind enemy lines, by parachute and glider. Now fighting under the command of BG James Gavin, the 82nd captured key river and canal bridges in the vicinity of Nijmegen. This was the division's fourth and last airborne assault of the war. December, the division was directed to move from base camp to the Ardennes region in Belgium, where the Germans had broken through the American lines. This began the Battle of the Bulge, a titanic struggle which saw the 82nd successfully oppose elite German armor divisions in the fight to restore the American battle lines.

1945: The new year began with the 82nd's defeat of the German 62nd Volksgrenadier and 9th Panzer Divisions and the capture of some 2,500 prisoners. By the end of January, All-American troopers penetrated the Seigfried defense line and attacked into Germany, fighting fierce battles with the enemy until late February. Late March saw the 82nd begin the final campaign of the war which culminated on 2 May with the surrender of the German 21st Army to then MG Gavin - 145,000 enemy troops and all their equipment. From July to December, the 82nd occupied Berlin, earning the nickname "America's Guard of Honor" from General George Patton.

1946: 12 January, the 82nd marched down Fifth Avenue in New York City in a colossal WW II Victory celebration. The Division then returned to Fort Bragg.

505th PARACHUTE INFANTRY REGIMENT
The regiment was activated at Fort Benning, Georgia on 6 July 1942. Unlike two of the three parachute regiments activated prior to the 505 by building onto or by splitting existing battalions, the 505 was formed from scratch. The great majority of the officers and men came direct from the Parachute School. Nick-named the PANTHERS because of the animal's speed, courage and fighting ability, the regimental patch was designed around this concept. The regiment's motto was READY.

The history of the regiment cannot be recounted without highlighting its commander, James Maurice Gavin - known as "Slim Jim". He was tall, slim, athletic, handsome and brilliant. Gavin had been an instructor at West Point and volunteered for paratrooper training in August, 1941. Later, he joined the Airborne Headquarters Staff and wrote the first manual for the employment of airborne forces. Upon activation of the 505th, Gavin was given command and promoted to full colonel at the young age of 35.

The 505 was probably the best-trained and most highly-motivated regiment in the Army. One 82nd Division staffer stated, "They were awesome, every man a clone of the CO and tough - not just in the field but 24 hours per day. Off duty, they'd move into a bar in little groups and if everyone there didn't get down on their knees in adoration, they'd simply tear the place up. Destroy it. God help the "straight legs"* they came across. They were a pack of jackals."

Gavin set a tough example for the men to follow - even doing free falls out of planes, rather than using the static line. He also expected a great deal from his officers. One young officer, reporting to him for the first time recalled, "Gavin looked at me and snarled, 'So you're an officer, huh? In this outfit that means you are first out the door of the plane and last in the chow line. Understand!?'"

On 12 February 1943, the order was received to move the regiment to

Fort Bragg to form the 505 Combat Team consisting of the 456th Parachute Field Artillery Battalion, elements of the 307 Airborne Engineers, 307 Airborne Medics and 80th Anti-Aircraft Battalion. On that same day, the Combat Team was assigned to the 82nd Airborne Division. The 505, along with these elements, accomplished every mission put before them.

*Paratroopers tucked their pants into their jump boots -blousing them out - "baggy pants". Thus, non-jumpers were called "straight legs" because they, of course, did not do this.

JUMP TRAINING

If a trooper wasn't unique prior to entering Airborne, the training he received took up the slack. Do you remember those first days of Jump School at Fort Benning? You were checked in and given a physical. Push-ups probably began immediately. Do you remember "pushing down Georgia" or "one more for Airborne"? Were you constantly challenged to perform your push-ups one handed?

Airborne training began with 'Stage A' and proceeded from there.

STAGE A: Shown a German paratrooper training film - eight hours of physical training with everything done at double time - exercises, running, rope climbing, judo, grass crawls, log tossing, Indian Clubs, obstacle course.

STAGE B: Four hours of physical training in the morning; but in the afternoon, true airborne training - Fuselage Prop: stand up on the mock plane, hook-up static line, check equipment of man in front, responding to the commands of jumpmaster, making a proper exit. Landing Trainer: student hooked up in a jumper's harness attached to a roller that slid down a long incline. Mock-up Tower: 381 platform with a long cable extending on an incline to a big, soft pile of sawdust. Trainasium: 401 maze of bars, catwalks, ladders. Free Towers: 250' tower for making controlled and free jumps. Wind Machine: practice rolling chutes.

STAGE C: Four hours of physical training in the morning. In the afternoon, instruction at the Packing Shed.

STAGE D: Five qualifying jumps from an actual C-47 in flight.

Upon completion, graduation from Jump School and the pinning of those coveted wings upon your uniform.

How did it feel to make that first qualifying jump? General Matthew Ridgway (first commanding general of the 82nd Airborne Division) said, "When the static line ripped the chute open, it was like the blow of a club across the shoulders. There followed a wonderful silence, but not for long. The ground rushed up at alarming speed. The landing impact was about like jumping off the top of a freight car traveling at 35 m.p.h. onto a hard, clay roadbed."

106

APPENDIX K
Gliders

As part of the Airborne forces, paratroopers were volunteers. Gliders were also a part of this new force, however, gliderists were not volunteers. Unfortunately for many units, outfits were designated as glider (both infantry and artillery) and included in this new Airborne Army. To the dismay of many paratroopers, a ride in a glider was, at some point, inevitable. Thus, a brief history on gliders.

Gliders were designed to be towed into combat by the C-47 and were nearly as large as the craft towing them. The American version - the WACO CG4A - was manned by a pilot and co-pilot and fitted with a swinging nose section to facilitate loading and unloading cargo. It had a payload of nearly 4,000 pounds and could carry 15 soldiers or six soldiers and a jeep or a wheeled gun.

The theoretical advantages of the glider were several - it could air-land ordinary infantrymen, who did not require the long, expensive training of paratroopers, directly into enemy-held territory. It eliminated the possible landing injuries that paratroopers were prone to sustain. It could put a full squad down on the ground closely bunched in one place, eliminating the forming up delays of paratroopers, and bring light artillery and weapons, or radio-equipped jeeps directly to the battlefield.

In field tests, gliders proved to be far more difficult and dangerous than envisioned. Although the WACO bad a strong frame of small gauge tubular steel and a sturdy plywood floor (the whole covered with aircraft fabric), the gliders were structurally flimsy, unarmed and unarmored. Thus, they were utterly defenseless against enemy ground or air attack. They weren't difficult to fly, but once cut loose from the tow ship, everything about the descent and landing had to be perfect. There was no second chance. Landing areas had to be smooth or there was usually a disastrous crash landing in a heavily-loaded vehicle not designed to withstand severe stress.

Most paratroopers - and gliderists - harbored a dread of gliding. Posters went up on barracks' walls in the glider regiments with a montage of photos of crashed gliders captioned: "Join the Glider Troops! No Flight Pay. No Jump Pay. But Never A Dull Moment!" Someone even wrote a song aptly expressing the feelings of the men: "Once I was Infantry. Now I'm a dope, riding gliders attached to a rope. Safety in landing is only a hope, and the pay is exactly the same."

Later, gliderists would receive the same additional pay as the paratroopers.

APPENDIX L
Panzer Ersatz und Ausbildungs Abteilung 100

The Panzer unit faced by the troopers of the 82nd Airborne Division in Normandy was the Panzer Ersatz und Ausbildungs Abteilung 100. The Abteilung was formed in April 1941 as a training unit, getting new recruits inside of tanks without tying down front line panzers. The unit had to make due with whatever tanks it could be spared. By the time the Abteilung collided with Gavin's men on 6 June, its TO & E consisted of a motley collection of French armor of the Hotchkiss and Renault marks, plus one Somua. Theoretically, one Panzer III (likely of Battle of France 1940 vintage) was on the unit strength chart. See the TO & E table for a breakdown of the composition of the Abteilung on D-Day.

The Germans made some efforts to improve these tanks. In 1940, the French tanks were helpless in the face of German tactical superiority, much of it due to the use of radio communications between the Panzers, in 1940. The French tanks were radioless. The French tanks in German service were retrofitted with radios, and a 2 meter rod aerial on the front fender. The commander's cupola was modified with a German split hatch. And in the case of the 37mm gun, a recent piece of information based on German records is that an Armor Piercing Composite Rigid, or "Arrowhead" round was developed and provided for this weapon. The round was not a success. Despite the harder warhead on the APCR round compared to the standard solid shot ammunition, low muzzle velocity led it to shatter upon impact with Allied armor plate.

With only these minor improvements and limited combat experience against the *Maquis*, the Abteilung, consisting of some 25 operational Panzers was sent to Normandy in May 1944. Under the command of Major Bardenschlager, the Abteilung was deployed between Carentan and Ste. Mere Eglise. The unit was tactically responsible to Infantrie Division 91, which covered the central portion of the Cotentin Peninsula. There was little time for additional training, the men of the unit joined French laborers in the frenzied construction of *Rommelspargel*— Rommel's Asparagus—glider impediments ordered planted in the fields in the final weeks before D-Day.

Oberleutnant Weber, in charge of 1. Kompanie, is quoted reassuring his men on the night of 5 June that the tracers that lit the sky seeking the Allied aircraft were, 'Zirkus! Nicht für uns bestimmt.' It was only a circus display, not to worry. Men of the unit went about their business, apparently unconcerned, the following morning. It would be the unfortunate fate of the poorly trained and armed Abteilung to face one of the most combat-ready units in all the Allied armies; the 505th Regimental Combat Team was a veteran unit whose men saw action in Sicily and Italy, during their combats jump during July and September 1943. On the morning of 6 June, 1944 parachutes were seen hanging from the trees and the fields were dotted with the wreckage of Allied gliders. The invasion had begun!

Weber would be proved wrong and his life cut short by the very paratroopers that came to Normandy during his 'circus display'. During his normal rounds on the morning of 6 June Weber was killed. Meanwhile, dispatch riders raced around the unit. No radios were used. The Abteilung did not go over to battle readiness until 9.00 a.m. Major Bardenschlager promptly set off from the Château de Francquetot, toward headquarters of Infantrie Division 91 about a kilometer away, in Houtteville. He was never seen again (This command paralysis also affected the unit the Abteilung was attached to; the commander, General Wilhelm Falley, was also killed by paratroopers before ever returning to his HQ from the exercise in Rennes).

After losing two important leaders, the unit was collected during the evening of 6 June to form a roadblock across the N803 running from Baupte to Carentan. The following morning the unit was sent piecemeal to various parts of the Cotentin front. No. 1 Platoon of 1. Kompanie went towards St. Lô and No. 2 toward Carentan. We now know the unit engaged the men of the 82nd Airborne Division in their strongholds along the Merderet River in the days that followed.

The Abteilung would be decimated during the Normandy battles. With so few tanks on its roster, and no replacements to be had, the Panzer Ersatz und Ausbildings Ateilung 100 was reduced to the on-paper strength of an anti-tank company. Its sole anti-tank weaponry was the panzerfaust and the remaining Panzer soldiers made their way on bicycles. On 7 July, OB West disbanded the unit.

TO & E of Panzer Ersatz und Ausbildings Abteilung 100 on 6 June 1944

Battalion HQ   5 x 35R

Sicherung Platoon   3 x 35R

1. Kompanie
    1st Platoon
    1 x Pz III (mark D?)
    4 x Pzkw 38H (Hotchkiss 35H)

    2nd Platoon
    1 x Pzkw B-2 (Renault B1-bis)
    4 x Pzkw 38H (Hotchkiss 35H)

3rd Platoon
1 x 35-S (Somua 35)
4 x 35R (Renault R-35)

2. Kompanie
    1st Platoon
    5 x 35R (Renault R-35)

THE MAPS (All US Army)

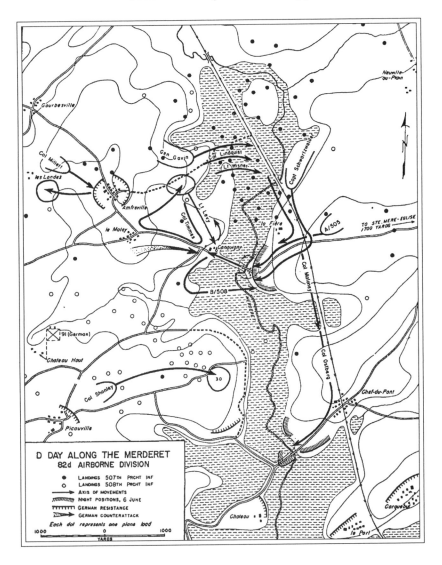

D DAY ALONG THE MERDERET
82d AIRBORNE DIVISION

- LANDINGS 507TH PRCHT INF
- LANDINGS 508TH PRCHT INF
→ AXIS OF MOVEMENTS
NIGHT POSITIONS, 6 JUNE
GERMAN RESISTANCE
GERMAN COUNTERATTACK

Each dot represents one plane load

1000   0   1000
YARDS

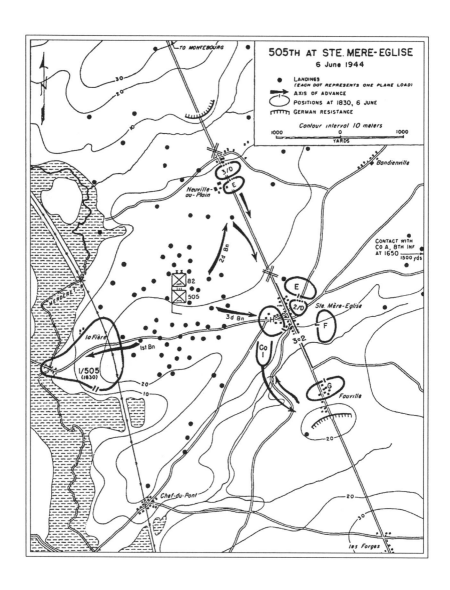

505TH AT STE. MERE-EGLISE
6 June 1944

● LANDINGS
(EACH DOT REPRESENTS ONE PLANE LOAD)
➤ AXIS OF ADVANCE
⬭ POSITIONS AT 1830, 6 JUNE
⬚⬚⬚ GERMAN RESISTANCE

Contour interval 10 meters

1000   0   1000
YARDS

TO MONTEBOURG

Bandienville

Neuville-
ou-Plain

3/0

E

2d Bn

82

505

3d Bn

la Fière

1st Bn

1/505
(1830)

CONTACT WITH
CO A, 8TH INF
AT 1650
1500 yds

E

2/0

Ste. Mère-Eglise

H

F

3=2

Co
I

G

Fauville

Chef-du-Pont

les Forges

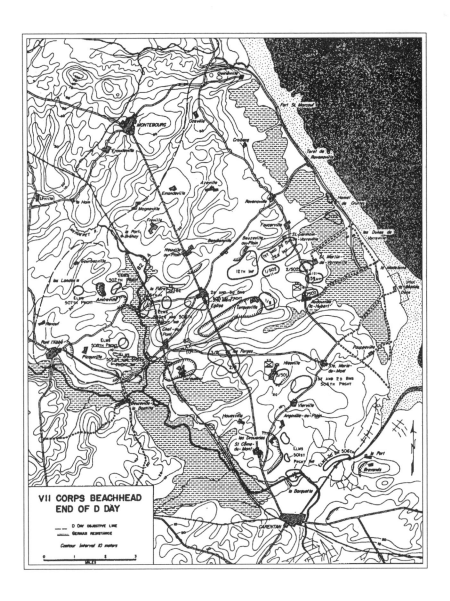

VII CORPS BEACHHEAD
END OF D DAY

- - - D Day objective line
.... German resistance

Contour interval 10 meters

0   1   2   3
MILES

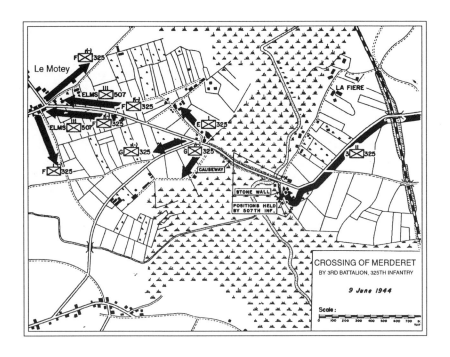

Le Motey

F⊠325

ELMS⊠507

ELMS⊠507

F⊠325

F⊠325

E⊠325

G⊠325

G⊠325

F⊠325

3⊠325

LA FIERE

CAUSEWAY

STONE WALL

POSITIONS HELD
BY 507TH INF.

CROSSING OF MERDERET
BY 3RD BATTALION, 325TH INFANTRY

9 June 1944

Scale :
0 100 200 300 400 500 600 700 YDS

113

THE PHOTOS

Pathfinder Team, 1st Battalion, 505th Parachute Infantry Regiment, 82nd AB Divi-
seen here on June 5, 1944 prior to boarding C-47s for their drop behind Utah Beach
hor second row, third from right in 'war paint').

gliders (right and above right) that had rough landings in the *Bocage* of Normandy.

The Gliderman's badge.

The 82nd Air-
borne patch.

The author at Camp Croft, N.C
November 1942 (age 17).

The author (right) January 1943—5th jump quali-
fied paratrooper, age 17 (Author's note:
paratrooper's wings belong on the left breast pocket
area!)

Photo taken June 4, 1944 in Grantham, England (author standing second from right
These paratroopers are all men from the original U.S. Army experimental Pathfinde
Team formed, in November 1943.

The author peeling a potato on KP' Duty at Camp Croft, January 1943.

The author (left) and Frank Bilick (D/505) at the reunion jump-in, June 3, 1994.

The first civilian jump back into Ste. Mere Eglise by D-Day veterans Bob Murphy (right) and John F. Lee (middle in photo).

Robert M. Murphy, finishing Jr. Year at Roslindale High School, May 1942. The author enlisted in the U.S. Army October 1, 1942.

The 505 PIR Base Camp 'tent-city' at Quorn, England, May 1944 (author was age 18).

A youthful General Jim Gavin. It was commonplace for Gavin to do heavy physical work the same as an enlisted man.

Lt. Colonel Benjamin H. Vandervoort pictured awaiting the flight to Normandy.

The author, now a combat veteran seen above in Garibaldi Square, October 1, 1943 at the surrender of Naples.

Generalleutnant Wilhelm Falley, commanding officer of the 91. Luftlande-Division was killed as he rode in his staff car toward headquarters by 82nd paratrooper Malcom D. Brannen, the commander of HQ Company, 3rd Battalion, 508th P.I.R.

Major Frederick C. A. Kellam, commander of 1st Battalion, 505th P.I.R., was nicknamed "Jack of Diamonds". Kellam was killed at la Fiére during the afternoon of June 6th attempting to recover some ammunition.

General Matthew Bunker Ridgeway, commanding general of the 82nd Airborne, landed by parachute with the 505th P.I.R. on D-Day.

A S.O.M.U.A. S-35 tank in German service before D-Day. This was one of the types faced by the men of the 82nd AB.

LE MOTEY CAUOUIGNY AMFREVILLE

LA FIERE CAUSEWAY. *Merderet River is in foreground.*

The Leroux *Manoir* house and outbuildings, seen here in 1997, are just as they were in 1944. The blown-out wall near the front door has been repaired.

Yves (right) and Chantal Poisson purchased the Leroux Manoir in 1973 and welcome all 82nd veterans to stay in one of their two guest rooms (telephone: 33413177).

Author Murphy (right), High School Hurdle Champion shows his mettle in race at Camp Croft, November 1942 (note guy on left is racing with a cigarette in his mouth!)

Casualties were high among men coming in by glider. Above are American casualties who died in the crash-landing of their glider near Ste. Marie du Mont.

The 'Iron Mike' statue at la Fiére.

An 'All American' platoon leader calls a HQ meeting in the field 'somewhere in Normandy' on June 6, 1944.

Four members of the 82nd Airborne enter Ste. Mere Eglise on
June 6, 1944.

A member of the 82nd Airborne
engages French children during
a brief lull in the fighting.

The 'little' bridge over the Merderet at la Fiére, seen
in a 1997 photo. Almost nothing has changed here
since WW II.

Soldiers of the 82nd (at left) Airborne used local horses to patrol
the streets of Ste. Mere Eglise.